ACKNOWLEDGMENTS

My mother worked very hard on getting this book to print, learning how to use the Programs on Amazon and to format the document for publication.

Laura Smith always helped me with the mechanics of posting.

Lisa commented on each post before I posted it.

Laura Denton also gave editorial comments on each post.

Loyal readers keep me going. These include friends and family here in Seattle and all over the world, especially my father and mother and many people at Williams & Connolly LLP in Washington DC.

A Fortunate Man with MS

Gil Greenman

DEDICATION

This Book is Dedicated to My Wise and Beautiful Wife,
Dr. Lisa Hebner Vila.

CONTENTS

Dedication
Acknowledgments
Introduction

Introduction

A resilient and determined man, I am "A fortunate man with MS."

After surviving a risky childhood in West Virginia, I graduated in the top 10% of my class from the Harvard Law school. Then I worked at the Washington DC law firm Williams and Connolly on cases that included the second impeachment trial in American history as the firm defended President Bill Clinton.

This book chronicles my life with multiple sclerosis.

MS entered my life when I was 26.

In 2014 I started my blog: A Fortunate Man with MS. This memoir brings the blog posts together in one place.

The story of the effect of MS on my life will, post by post, play out here in this memoir. This is one story of one person with multiple sclerosis, a very fortunate person.

All or nearly all of the people who live with multiple sclerosis, and the myriad angels who care for them will tell you that if you have met one person with multiple sclerosis, you have met precisely one person with multiple sclerosis. Just as nature has decided to make snowflakes different, the stories of people with MS are every one of them very different.

My goal is to tell a good story without judgment. This story will attempt to avoid judgment, expressed or implied (I am a lawyer), of anyone else suffering from multiple sclerosis, including the author and of any of the characters in the story.

I understand that this is an impossible goal, but it is the goal nonetheless.

There are many things that this memoir is not. It is not a medical resource. It will not catch you up on the latest treatments. I have in my twenty years since diagnosis sought whatever the latest treatment was that had been approved by the fallible authority of the FDA. It is not a self-help blog. There is no list of tips or checklists. It is not a scientific or factual resource. It will not contain statistics, and it will not pretend to take even the smallest step into the wealth of knowledge that the angels who research, tend, love, and care for the people with multiple sclerosis have accumulated over countless years of grappling with this chronic illness. These angels know best that it is "our" MS, and I would never presume to describe the learning they have carved out of their struggles.

This is my story, told in the hope that maybe just one person who has been recently diagnosed or has lost hope might read it. Maybe they will take just one more walk, go to one more work out, move one step away from despair, or strive for one more day.

2014

The Beginning of the Story

At 9 years old, standing on the ice in the middle of the partly frozen river, I realized this was a big mistake. As my more sensible older brother watched from the bank, our friend Jeff had led me out near the middle of the wide Kanawha, an industrial strength river on which coal barges steamed through the West Virginia valley. It had never frozen before to my knowledge.

A man stopped his car in a traffic lane of the narrow interstate overpass a bit upstream. He got out, waved his arms and shouted "YOU DAMN KIDS, GET OFF THAT RIVER!!"

Hearing him yell and seeing him risking his own life, it all suddenly dawned on me. We were within 20 yards of the middle stream of unfrozen river where the dark brown water rushed by. Looking at the water, the overpass, and the distance to the bank, I realized that we had made an awful mistake. Before that moment, it frankly had not entered my 9-year-old mind.

Living a block from the bank of the Kanawha, our parents

had made very clear that we were never to go down the steep bank, let alone approach the fast water. A handful of kids drowned every year, and my usually cheery mother made a point of showing me the newspapers describing their deaths: 'Ricky Stubbs, 7 years old, drowned in Kanawha'. Now here I was, the young follower of 14-year-old Jeff, looking back at the bank toward my brother. Those were the longest 50 steps of my life — filled with the sound of the ice crunching under my feet on each step. But since I am here telling this, you can assume correctly that the ice never cracked and broke, sending us down, swiftly under and gone. We survived and soon had to confess to relieved but furious parents after a neighbor turned us in.

Terrible judgment saved by plain dumb luck stands as one of many ways that I have been a very fortunate man, a man who in 17 years, having survived the river, would find himself diagnosed with multiple sclerosis.

All of us are born with and develop unique gifts in this fragile human life. Chronic illness, in my case multiple sclerosis, refracts our gifts, distorting and sending our light into unexpected directions. In my case, mercifully, multiple sclerosis did not impact my life with a force that snuffed out the development of gifts or the enjoyment of life. It came at the crest of a first wave of long-sought success.

The Fall

Free fall. This. Is. Free fall.

The precipice had been lofty and the stuff of my dreams. My new cavernous corner office, complete with leather couch, brown wood, and oriental carpet, spoke to teenage fantasies inspired while nerding out on PBS's Paper Chase series with John Houseman as Kingsfield, the terrifying Harvard Law professor. My own Harvard Law School diploma on the wall and success at the firm had kept me on track with my partnership class and finally landed this corner with a separate office for my secretary.

What's more, I had just begun work on another case for one of the most respected and formidable lawyers of his generation, the senior member of a group of professional fathers whose trust in me I had spent fourteen years trying to honor.

I had arrived. Truly, finally, and for my goals, completely, arrived.

Only to plummet headfirst off the edge of the cliff. I saw my whole life rushing up to swallow everything.

All of it. Going. Going.

Of course, this wasn't an event occurring in a single instant. Much of it had been long in coming, but like a frog in slowly warming water, the entirety of my situation had not yet pierced my grandiose denial.

There had been hints of a change, moments where I wondered, "does this lawyer think I am making sense?" "Do they think I understand what I am saying?" Of course, every professional daily risks appearing incompetent, but was I? Sadly, the 23 excellent years of law school, clerkships, and success at the firm provided less and less, and finally, no comfort at all. My long history of pushing through MS exacerbations, cheerfully making adaptations like using a cane, and working at the pace of a DC litigator came to an end when the one muscle I could not circumvent or supplement failed — my brain.

One Friday found me sitting in my office working on a draft letter. Actually, it was more like a paragraph, some specific language on a topic for which I had the most knowledge on the team.

The time had moved on to 8 pm, and I still sat, reading the same background — emails and articles and cases and prior letters — over and over. Their language did not seem to stick in my head, and I could not piece things together into that arc of words that had always sprung out of me after enough reading and thinking. Instead, anxiety conquered my old steady ground like an invading horde. Retreating in disarray, my concentration moved every minute to another email or a completely different topic, even subjects having nothing to do with work.

One of the subjects causing distraction was a phone call I had received from an employee of the local boutique bank that held the mortgage on my townhouse in fashionable Old Town, Alexandria. Was I aware, he asked, that my mortgage, obtained in the go-go early 2000s, was a balloon note that came due in three months? "No, seriously, in three months, you owe us $700,000." I had planned to refinance soon when I had originally taken out the loan, but 2008 and also a great (meaning awful) personal recession had intervened, as well as several years of separation, divorce, and a recent shifting of house ownership back to me in exchange for a large payment toward a new house for my kids' mother.

"No Mr. Banker, I had quite forgotten that I owed you $700,000 in a few weeks. Thanks so much for your call." So, you see, on that fateful Friday evening, my mind would also occasionally wander to the detailed financial application for mercy I was to submit to the bank the following Monday.

Soon it was 8:30 pm, and I was no further along with the letter for my case. "Ok, once more to the breach. One more stab at a sentence," I said to myself in an Eeyore voice, that is, if Eeyore had just been swept up in an overwhelming invasion of the Hundred Acre Wood.

Then the phone rang.

The phone call was my kids' mother calling with my son to say that Bonnie had been hit by a car. Bonnie was their Scotty puppy dog, now three years old. They were just driving home from the veterinarian and trying to figure out how they were going to tell my twin girls who were nine at the time and loved Bonnie.

I said how sorry I was. I sat and thought of sad kids and poor Bonnie, then folded my tent and went home to return early Saturday and press on.

The rest of the weekend flew by in an excruciating mix of fretful activity and complete lack of progress. By Sunday night, I knew that this was not writer's block, or merely anxious overwhelm. These were old friends to a lawyer used to pressure and family stress and writing for a living. And though my historically under-confident, self-critical adolescent voice carped about my laziness and lack of focus, even I could hear the adolescent carping as bringing a knife to a gunfight.

This was different. I was different. Something had gone wrong. I faced the moment I had long dreaded – raising my hand at my firm and saying to my partners that something was wrong with my ability to do my job. I had skated by it, jumped over it, and otherwise avoided this moment at both close quarters and happy long distance. It was over, finally over, and after the long weekend of Bonnie, the mortgage, and the unwritten paragraph, I could not pretend otherwise. If I tried, events would rush in to write the story for me, and this outcome could not be allowed to happen. Staring one last time at my desk full of photos and my beautiful office in my wonderful firm, I said goodbye to that life out loud.

Monday morning found me in the senior partner's office explaining that something was wrong. Without hesitation, he said that health was the most important thing and that I should take some time off, get tested, work with the Executive Director and firm resources, and come back with a plan that made sense for me. As I spoke the death sentence of my former life and he responded with compassion, the free fall jolted and changed.

I wish I could say that a billowy parachute opened up with the letter "G" on it and floated me easily groundward. Nope. It was more like an old chute full of holes, plus a bunch of bats and buzzards and garbage floated out in a twisting trail as I zig-zagged back and forth in a slower descent. Appointments, meetings with bankruptcy lawyers and financial advisors, psychiatrists, all followed.

But my head had stopped hurtling into the center of my life, for now. This fortunate man could breathe again, because after that weekend, the end of a crescendo, I had walked away.

Laughing and Connected

Like many last week, some of my time went to watching Robin Williams' movies and his 2002 HBO stand-up special, which for me represents the single funniest 90 minutes of raw(!!) comedy ever aired. With his everyman looks, he could make connections in the deep and shallow, the big and small, and between us all. He taught me and many of us who crested our teenage years wide-eyed at the glory that was cable TV. He taught us what was funny, and what was funny went beyond silly, though there was plenty of silly, and improvisation. In so many sad and comic and moving ways, he showed us how connected we all truly are, knitting it across frame after frame of a massive body of work. Mozart died at 36. How lucky are we to have had almost three extra decades of our own Mozart in Robin Williams?

One of my friends in college resembled a young Robin Williams. While never aspiring to professional comedy, Eli shared his easy love of laughter with us all in our freshman dorm and on the rugby team. We are still in touch, and the week spent thinking of Williams also brought up for me one of my favorite and, to me, important laughs with Eli.

A couple months after graduation from college found me living with a girlfriend in a tiny apartment in the basement of a row house. She had left town for a couple of nights, and Eli needed a place to stay. We woke up the first morning to the girlfriend's alarm clock. Having become used to the sound, I hardly noticed it anymore, but Eli was horrified. The clock emitted an electronic beeping version of the first movement of Vivaldi's 4 Seasons:

Da Dum Dum Dum Dada Daa! Dada Dum Dum Dum Dada Daa! (Listen online for the tune if this rendition is not adequate).

Trained in violin, Eli could not stand the conversion of Vivaldi to a series of electric beeps. He used the words "abomination" and "tragic," but said them as kindly as he could at 630am. That night we had some Chinese food and drank a few beers and talked about our boring first jobs out of college. We touched on long term goals, having some idea we'd both be some sort of professionals.

Then suddenly Eli smiled and said, "But we do know one thing! We know that at 6:30am tomorrow we will hear — Da Dum Dum Dum Dada Daa! Dada Dum Dum Dum Dada Daa!"

We laughed hard. Then one of us added: "And off he goes on the train to work. Works all day. Train home. G'night honey…

Da Dum Dum Dum Dada Daa! Dada Dum Dum Dum Dada Daa!"

We were laughing really hard now.

"Then the weekend comes! Mow. Mow. Mow. Rake. Rake. Rake. G'night honey. . .

Da Dum Dum Dum Dada Daa!"

Crying laughing, we continued: "Add kids to the weekend! Soccer. Soccer. Goal! Clap. Clap. Clap. G'night honey…

Da Dum Dum Dum Dada Daa!

That is our lives for the next 40 years!"

We have laughed about that riff ever since. For a second, it didn't matter that we had little idea what we would do all day at work. That night, the arc of our adult lives seemed to stretch in a comically predictable and somewhat poignant line, punctuated each morning by a truly obnoxious alarm clock. I am so grateful for such a friend and moment, sitting there on the brink of our next chapters.

Another dear friend recently asked me after my first post here what I wanted from this blog. Below is my on-the-fly reply, and as I think of Robin Williams and the chapters that unfolded after the laugh with Eli back in 1989, all that I hope is to knit my one small frame of the enormous story that ultimately connects us all:

"What I want I tried to signal in the Introduction. I want to tell an interesting story about a person who made a beautiful life not only in spite of but even because of his disease. I want to talk about relationships and mistakes and how I believe some of my psychological deficits led to the disease coming to save me from myself. I want to tell stories about a big career and a wonderful quieter life that is even more rich, rewarding, and exciting. I want to talk about duties to self and to others and loving and kindness and manipulation and darkness and the unfailing kindness of strangers and the stories people tell to a wobbly well-dressed youngish man with a cane and sometimes with a gorgeous stylish wife next to him and other times alone or with a wicked cute dog. I want the story to continue and grow as I am and be connected as we all are."

HEAT

1914. Somewhere in France …

All he could hear was the raspy chop, chop, chop of the machine gun and the sickening thud of its shells hitting the dead bodies of his two best friends. Joking just before, the three of them had been hit almost immediately after the call to charge. Now he was trapped. Their company's deep, safe, straight trench was fifty yards away. Hit on his left leg, he couldn't make that in one go, but he could not stay. He thought he had seen a shell hole nearby, so he made the move. Lurching low he fell with brief gratitude into the hole, but instead of relief he found mustard gas! It lingered from an earlier gas attack. He inched back up the hole as high as he could.

Oh god! Gasmask. Can't reach it. Must move gear to get to

it. Stretching up. Sharp pain. Black.

A bullet saved him from the gas. He joined his two friends.

My imagined trenches were the long straight grooves between the cinderblocks in the wall of the school nurse's office. Lying on the old vinyl nurse cot, I traced story after story on the wall, foxholes big and small in the cinderblocks. At nine, my fascination with military history bordered on obsession. My desire to leave class due to "illness" crossed the border into annoying. One day my father arrived and kindly but firmly put a stop to me faking sick. I shipped back to school, leaving the battlefield behind. I would give anything now for my illness to be a nine-year-old's fake.

Heat is my mustard gas. Any foxhole – any room or car or space I enter - is scary for a few seconds. Getting stuck in heat starts to melt me like frosty the snowman trapped in the greenhouse. Weakness, numbness, pain, chest-tightening, and blackouts may follow, depending on the temperature. If I rush to escape or reach my gear, I may fall. I suddenly go from light-hearted to scared and then frustrated and dark. It's hard for people besides my friends and family to understand. To my loved ones, I shake my head and say, "I melted."

Walking into any new space, I am always thinking, "How hot is it?"

Shit, it's too hot (anything above 69 degrees Fahrenheit). Can I leave? Where is my kit with cold packs? Oh God.

It happens in an instant, and the fear is always there, mostly in summer, where even air conditioning does not completely solve it. In summer's office elevators, the AC always weakens, and I can feel the heat off the bodies of the people who just survived the walk outside. When I start my car in summer, the two to three minutes before cooling are hell.

In winter, rooms get overheated, and here we are again. Do I wear a suit jacket? A sweater? Probably never.

And yes, I have equipment. And yes, I sometimes get ahead of the heat and ride it out. But it is always there, and life does not always unfold in slow easy stages. I don't know what would happen if I got stuck in heat without relief, like if, for example, a car ran out of gas in summer sun. I just don't know.

Compared to my many symptoms, including loss of most of my walking and some of my good mind, the heat is my great war. World War II may follow, but that's another day.

MS and the Buddha

Go slow

Please go slow

Constant reminder

Of change

Of impermanence

Chronic dissatisfaction could engulf compassion

Manage loss

Grieve like a Buddha

Laugh like a Buddha

And sit

And stand, if you can

My hands do not really touch

My legs do not really walk

But my eyes see

My ears hear and

Sometimes even listen

My voice speaks

My tongue tastes

 I am alive

And Dying

As are we all

Community of Now

As he spoke the pain of his wife's long struggle with seizure medication in and out of nursing homes good and bad, Bud's face was etched with his long stoic life. His early years in the blazing sun and freezing cold of Eastern Washington, the Korean war, and almost 60 years of marriage to the wife he adored and had just buried in a swirl of grief and relief. After his story trailed into the now familiar endgame of self-deprecating jokes and sturdy answers to my expression of concern, he went back to tending his flowers in front of his tiny old house, and I continued my slow walk up the hill with the dog.

Life's chapters hold varied communities for each of us. At each stage we can ask "Who are my people?" The community of now for me is rich, worthy of the savoring I have time to lavish on it, and far from the blizzard of briefs and billables left behind in Washington. It is only missing one crucial part, leaving a huge hole that has the effect of widening my community to thousands, but only for a constant stream of fleeting, painful moments. Come with me for a few more snapshots of now.

In front of a fire, with smiles, good wine and wit, the friends sat and shared the latest ironic moments of their lives. This was one of several such gatherings at this elegant home with some of our people — fabulous hostess-chef and seeker Julia and salt-of-earth, wise fellow travelers Meg and Steve who have adopted us into their huge, warm Seattle family.

My wife addressed Davey the host, who had a magical ability to continuously fill up all wine glasses. "It was sweet running into you this morning at your regular coffee stop and seeing you talk to all the regulars by name, like the old man at the table who looked like a veteran." Davey chuckled and said that when in town his coffee routine never varies and that he enjoys the regulars but not his fellow range rover captains.

I said, "You know, guys, in my neighborhood I am one of those guys who 'the Daveys' say hi to. You know, the one who's always around, talking to Bud his neighbor or at the coffee shop with his cane and the cute dog." And we laughed because it's true. I'm the guy you'll see lingering over coffee, talking or typing on his cell or having his dog do tricks for people, a piece of the local human furniture.

Another evening, I stood up after a long dinner at a

neighbor's house. Legs felt almost too stiff to walk, a recent downward trend. Sadness and fear rushed in, but they met a determination to walk up the hill with the dog. As the two of us walked up the hill, a dog buddy and the human she was walking appeared across the street. Jubilation for the dogs and a chat between us humans. Alex held onto both dogs as they strained to find a balance between getting up the hill to the park and playing with each other on the way. We talked about our summers, and then he took both dogs on a long walk while I made my way home slowly but with a smile and less stiffness.

Children fill much of my life these days. Wonderful children, growing into young women and men. None of them are in fact my own blood children now. Those are the three children who I can't reach at all. After so many lost years and moments that will never return, my grief leaves me wondering how it compares to the grief of parents whose children actually die.

Every child I see is one of my own children, at whatever the age of the child in front of me. Not just all amber haired girls around 14. My daughters are also the toddlers in among pumpkins at our local nursery. Not just the young man on his bike riding by. My son is on every field at any age and game, not figuratively, literally. Inside, my whole being lunges toward them as if they have come back somehow. A wave of anxious hope and joy that maybe the breach might all have been a bad dream. And then the fleeting waves of joy, some towering and some tiny, break upon reality's shore. Here I am, not the least bit alone but wholly and what seems forever without my three.

These are glimpses of part of what makes up my community of now. I am a fortunate man, incredibly fortunate to have my stepchildren close and open, blessed beyond words by an exquisite partner, and surrounded by wonderful friends. On most days I can even feel fortunate to have ever had years with my own children, years no one can take away. Years which in the now mean that my community includes every child, every single one, who is for just one bittersweet moment one of my own that I lost. This ownership of past and bittersweet mixture with all children now keeps the hole from widening.

And compared to my rich warm now of real people who I can see and hear and touch, the hole cannot possibly sink me. I have gone where the love is, the most fortunate of men.

I love now.

The Question

You have less than some and more than most what life will you make of this?

The Goal Is No Longer Health But Beauty

(from Santa Fe) My goal is no longer health. It is beauty. My health will eventually decline, but my openness and search for beauty in the world will only grow. I search to touch the anima mundi everywhere. Which is of course right here. Just here. Where I am sitting.

A Christmas Miracle

My home growing up had a playroom, a sunny place full of light where my older brother and I built castles and highways and dreams. Out the windows towered the high entrance of All Saints Episcopal Church, up a hill that seemed a mountain to me. We never took the steps, scrambling up and rolling down the hill. To us, the house and church made a playground. Classic preachers' kids, we often played hard and loudly. Wars with my arsenal of realistic plastic WWII firepower. And later, fire crackers. Snowballs at cars. When I returned to the church at 19, I realized that the entrance hill was less than ten feet tall.

Inside the church on Christmas Eve spread a sea of handheld candles flickering as we sang Silent Night. I often crept into the choir loft where my mother played the organ and I could look down across the candles and feel that perfect mix of anticipated presents and present anticipation of baby Jesus arriving.

One year, we could not afford a real tree. This was the early 70s, so fake trees looked like a stack of green pipe cleaners.

We soldiered on, reminded to be grateful by my parents' work with the one family at the church who truly had nothing. We'd be fine. I was fine. That is, so long as the one $12 toy choice from the JCPenney catalog I had picked showed up on Christmas Morning.

And then it happened, one Christmas Eve.

After the early service, I wandered back to our house to find something to do before the midnight show. I walked past the living room into the playroom, where I saw a dark fake tree and a bunch of boxes of ornaments and lights. I spun around to behold what had grown in the living room. Where our fake tree had been, now stood an enormous natural tree, decorated with beautiful new ornaments and bright lights. I can see it now, glistening with those fancy lights and shining globes.

I sat down on the footstool and just stared at it. After a few minutes, my dad walked in wearing his black priest shirt and white collar. "Gilbey, look at the tree." "Look at the tree." He would always chuckle telling this part of the story, because I was clearly looking at the tree, my face cupped in my hands and elbows pressed against my knees, just sitting there, looking.

When you're seven, that's a miracle.

I would later learn that someone in the choir had heard my mom mention the fake tree and had conspired with a lawyer in the choir to buy the real tree and gear and sneak it in while we were at the early service. Maybe that's where I learned lawyers earned money.

What I believed at seven was that Christmas is magical. Still do.

The Ghost of ChristMaS Presence

For most of us, including this fortunate, fortunate man, the holidays arrive with many guests at the house that is a soul. Rumi described these arrivals in his famous poem, *The Guest House*–

"This being human is a guest house. Every morning a new arrival.

A joy, a depression, a meanness, some momentary awareness comes as an unexpected visitor.

Welcome and entertain them all!

Even if they are a crowd of sorrows, who violently sweep your house empty of its furniture, still, treat guest honorably.

He may be clearing you out for some new delight.

The dark thought, the shame, the malice. meet them at the door laughing and invite them in.

Be grateful for whatever comes. Because each has been sent as a guide from beyond."

Triggered by a song or a scent, some of my holiday arrivals

are fond memories of childhood or moments with my own children filled with wonder. Some are warm conversations with friends or letters from all over about everyone's last year passed. And some others are moments of keen realization of loss and grief. Like Dickens's bountiful ghost of Christmas Present who arrives with the waifs of ignorance and want, the holidays can bring sad guests.

As I described in my post, "Community of Now," my distance from my own children colors life each day. This coloring deepens at Christmas, remembering the better times when they were young. Wide eyed wonder of a little boy opening his Tonka truck and of amber-haired twins rushing down in snuggly pajamas to behold a fire lit room awash in gifts. I will be forever grateful that I was relatively able when they were at the chasing, running, toddler ages. For now, all I can do is let the grief move through me and hope they have a happy Christmas in Virginia. Life is full of chapters. I try to stay hopeful and wait for someday.

As another year passes, the large greedy guest of MS also gets much louder. MS is that guest who was never invited and never leaves reliably. Sometimes he used to disappear, only to resurface at inconvenient times, demanding his steroid infusions. Now he "walks" with me every day, and I carry a cane to keep him under control. He's that guest that none of the others want to engage in conversation, and when he does speak, often the room goes quiet for a minute in discomfort or even horror.

Last year at a ski house with friends, I returned from a walk too long with no balance left and a face full of the ashen, drained frustration that overtakes the one who dares walk a few score paces beyond capacity. I remember the looks on my friends' faces as they offered the perfect mix of support without syrup, helping me find a chair in which to fall apart for a while. In that moment, I was the ghost of MS Presence. He cannot be banished, but he can rest if well-handled and supported.

At the close of 2014, as I inevitably compare how difficult getting somewhere this year was from last, my MS screams, "You can barely walk at all anymore!" He is an alarmist, this guest, but he is not completely wrong. My year of workouts aimed at creating a plateau where I lost no more of my last quarter mile of walking ability has not succeeded, and I worry that a blog post titled, "Is this the last year before the scooter?" may get written in 2015. As it approaches and I grow completely comfortable with things like wheelchairs in airports, I can feel a gradual acceptance mixed with the unfailing determination to keep up the pace on workouts. It will be what it will be.

And when my MS guest's voice gets too loud to bear, humor comes to the rescue. Movies like "Home for the Holidays" with Holly Hunter or anything with Chevy Chase remind that we are all ridiculous, all surrounded by wacky characters who can push our buttons, all beautifully broken together.

The perfect holiday is one where all the guests of the soul pile in but our acceptance of them leaves us able to be present and feel the magic of the moment. And then, a moment later, we stand gaping like the family in "A Christmas Story" as we watch the Bumpus hounds eating our turkey that had taken days to prepare. An hour later, we eat Chinese food and forever look back on it as a favorite Christmas. What we make of the MesS is what matters, always.

2015

**National
Multiple Sclerosis
Society**

On the Board

"When I had to leave legal practice in 2010, it was a very dark year. It was dark even though I had the support of my law firm and good disability insurance.   I wish everyone who goes through a dark moment because of MS could see this group today and all the work you are doing. Thank you for the honor of voting me onto the Board."

This is what I said to the Board of the Greater Northwest
Chapter of the National Multiple Sclerosis Society this
morning. A group of accomplished, dedicated people, they
all showed up at 7 am on a Saturday morning to spend
several hours discussing how to achieve more in the
movement to cure MS and support those who currently live
with MS. What a wonderful moment today was for this
fortunate man.

The Day We First Met and the Dance Began

There was nothing romantic about it. MS flirted with me on a long bike ride in Seattle in the summer of 1993. After the ride, I felt a strange sensation in my groin and upper thighs that lasted a few hours. A few months later, I fell hard on a slippery sidewalk in Boston's Back Bay. My legs and arms felt a weird numbness and tingling, a little like when your leg is on its way back from having fallen asleep.

I bounced from doctor to doctor at the university health services and finally ended up sitting with a deadpan neurologist. He'd sent me for a MRI.

"Your MRI shows several active lesions on your brain. What you have is clearly multiple sclerosis."

"What the hell is that?" screamed my mind. I knew in some calmer corner of my brain that it was one of those scary diseases with an acronym beginning with an "M" like muscular dystrophy or maximum meningitis or mega measles or multiple sclerosis or etc. etc. But those were just a bunch of letters and images of Jerry Lewis and his kids and . . . "What the hell?"

"The last law student I diagnosed with M.S. chose to lead a less stressful life. I think he is very happy and selling real estate on the North Shore (of Massachusetts)."

Now the doctor had my full attention. Looking back, it seems like that moment on the frozen river at 9 years old. My flailing fear gave way to ambition, just like it had to self-preservation and the slow, ice crunching under my feet walk when I was 9. I sat there looking at this man — some doctor, reading slides and telling me that it was over, that I should hang it up.

Not two years before, I had received my first set of law school grades and quietly enjoyed the fact that many of the people who had talked the most in class now fell silent. My grades encouraged more attempts at thoughtful comments, not less.

I had walked into a classroom to argue in the first-year moot court competition to find Archibald Cox sitting as one of the judges.

Archibald Cox!

One of the great heroes of the greatest generation, the paragon of virtue, the standard for all that was good and ethical and excellent in government, the man fired by Nixon. I argued well, and he said so. Archibald Cox, a living legend.

I had not come to Harvard Law School and moved within striking distance of this dream to hang it up. Not now.

"Doctor, with all due respect, I am not going to do that (downscale and de-stress). I come from a long line of ministers and teachers. I'm not going to hang it up. I'm going to clerk for a federal judge in Hawaii and then another in Seattle and then I'm going to work for a law firm and make some money and maybe do some good along the way." Looking back, this was one of the most important steps in my life.

"What else can you do for me doctor?"

"Steroid treatments."

Great. Steroids, like some roided out, washed up athlete?

"No, not those kinds of steroids. It is medicine, called Solu Medrol. It will help shorten and tamp down your exacerbations. You should start tomorrow with a five-day course of infusions. I will call health services."

The next morning found me in a hospital room taking off the watch with the face the color of the water around St. Thomas where I had bought it on my honeymoon not three weeks earlier. The kind nurses with the wicked 'Baahsten' accents stuck me with an IV needle FIVE TIMES AND COULD NOT FIND A VEIN. No IV. I lost it, storming out and demanded that they supply a surgeon the next morning. He was a young resident wearing the exact same watch I had on. He got the IV going on the first try, which I have now come to learn is exactly the opposite of how things usually go in the nurse/doctor world.

And life went on. I went to the Advanced Constitutional Law class taught by the legendary Lawrence Tribe. I tried to say smart things, and felt more or less ok, but never physically quite the same. My Relapsing Remitting MS more or less remitted, but honestly, I can't say my fingers and legs have ever felt quite mine again.

My eyes and ears sure worked though. I could see. I could hear Professor Tribe's reassuring voice in his office as he set up an appointment with a specialist at Mass General.

I stared at him in disbelief as he had his assistant TAKE A MESSAGE from Senator Lloyd Bentsen (democratic VP nominee and slayer in debate of Dan Quayle). Tribe would not interrupt our conversation for Lloyd Bentsen.

I graduated in the top 10% of my class from Harvard Law School. To this day, part of me still can't really believe that I even got in. I passed the bar in Seattle that summer with only one more steroid treatment. I clerked in Hawaii. I clerked in Seattle. And, fortunately, I did not hear from the MS much at all leading up to another pivotal moment.

In that crossroads moment fate firmly took the hand of this fortunate man. I had planned to practice law in Seattle and had accepted an offer for after my Seattle/9th Circuit clerkship from one of the best firms in town. One day the hiring partner called and said that he wanted me to know that they would no longer be honoring the years of clerkships with salary credit. In the big markets like New York and DC, they gave both salary credit and big bonuses for clerkships.

The same message in various versions came rushing to me. "Gather ye roses while ye may." "Carpe Diem." "If you are going to sell your soul, at least get a good price." "Money talks and bullshit walks." But the most memorable message came from a plainspoken Assistant U.S. Attorney who had befriended me in my first-year summer in Seattle and listened at lunches patiently three years later as I dithered over what to do. I had an offer from the formidable law firm of Williams & Connolly in Washington, DC. Going back and forth, my struggle boiled down to the question: "Should I go for it or should I play it safe?" At length he smiled and said: "You know, I think in life you only get one chance to play for the Yankees. If you don't take it, you'll always wonder."

In that moment I learned for the first time what I would see over and over in more than a decade of law practice – a well-placed one liner beats a 50-page brief. I also knew that I was going to trust that fortune favors the bold.

And fortune smiled. I still work in a limited role for this wonderful institution, and I packed what feels like a 40-year career into 14 years of practice that ended in 2010.

I left it all on the field, working 3000-hour years followed by long breaks, careening from periods of remission through attacks treated by Solu Medrol, and later by the new interferon drugs (in turn: Avonex, then Betaseron, then both

Betaseron and Copaxone – two shots a night, yay) and finally Tysabri, a monthly infusion. A long history of hard work earned the support of the firm and of good disability insurance which in the end saved me from the financial ruin that usually befalls the loss of the ability to do that job for which I had trained and dreamed of doing – being a lawyer.

I will never know whether my health would have been better in a less stressful job. I do know that to my dying day I will be grateful that I took my shot. It has landed me in a place where I still have a professional identity, some options, and am working to create a satisfying life now living with Secondary Progressive MS.

As it turned out, the first day I met MS was not the last day of anything. It is a dance where most days I still feel like I am leading, with new steps and challenge for every stage and tune.

Today I Bought a Wheelchair. It's Okay, and I May Even Walk More Because of It.

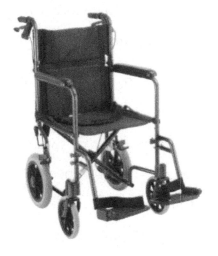

Sometimes what we dread can surprise us and turn around. My engagement with wheelchairs began about ten years ago with electric scooters in amusement parks. That didn't feel too bad, and back then it got you to the head of the line. It took me a long time to accept airport wheelchair service, and I am still not thrilled about being escorted by an always kind, hardworking soul in the airport. But because it helps so much, I finally stopped fighting it and have become used to it and to the sometimes-interesting conversations with folks. The idea of my own chair, however, has always felt like a big line which I needed to work hard not to cross. I thought about it as a true Rubicon, something to be dreaded, something to inspire action to avoid crossing that line.

But today, on this sunny day, Oscar the dog and I wandered into the well-appointed medical supply store that sits across from some of our favorite restaurants near our house.

There are walks out of my reach, but many times they would not be out of my reach if I could just sit for a bit. There are also walks with other people who could continue the walk with me sitting for a bit while they push. The arc of need and desire to keep walking led me this morning to look at what else might help, thinking it might be a light wheelchair with high enough arms to also serve as a walker. And Eureka! Of course, it exists. It's aluminum and folds up easily. It is a travel chair, not one you can wheel yourself. It has handbrakes on the comfortable handles. I don't know whether it will work as well as I hope, but we shall see. I am cancelling my electric scooter for the MS Walk in April. I will walk some of it, and, for some of it, my team, the GREEN MANiacs, will push.

Oscar liked the shop, and though he is afraid of luggage,

brooms, vacuums, and even large packages, he did not mind the wheelchairs at all. He received his usual attention and admiration from the salesman and customers. I pushed the chair around with Oscar. Then Bill, the salesman, pushed the chair around with me in it and Oscar alongside. The humans dealt with financial details, and Oscar and I left, looking forward to having a new friend in a few days.

Just like that. I own a wheelchair. Like my handsome canes, it may become a part of my look and my way. I may walk more because of it, or I may not. Either way, today it feels full of promise. Most important, it just feels okay.

Enormous Support at The Dinner of Champions

May 9, 2015

I was honored to speak at this wonderful event last Saturday, May 9 at the Four Seasons in Seattle. The text of my speech is below. The event raised more than a million dollars in one evening for the National MS Society's research and other programs. A video shown to the attendees ended with me saying, "I've been told by so many people who would know that there's no doubt MS can be solved, that the issue can be solved, it's just a matter of money. It's just that simple, and many things in life are like that and this is one of them." The first line of the speech picked up on that.

"It's true that many things in life are simple. Living with MS is definitely not one of them.

My journey with MS began in my mid-20s with numbness in my limbs. For the next several years, my relapsing-remitting MS didn't demand too much of me. When my symptoms would flare up, I'd hit them with steroids. When the first MS medications became available, they helped some, too.

As you saw in the video, my legal career took off. I was able to work on some of the most high-profile cases in the nation – to literally be part of history. But as my MS progressed, it became more and more difficult for me to keep up with the mental and physical demands of such a high-pressure job.

After working so hard and doing my best to cram a 40-year legal career into just 14 years… I made the difficult decision to step down from day-to-day litigation work and to leave my dream job as a partner at this amazing law firm – a place where some of the most powerful attorneys in the nation showed me the utmost compassion because, as they said, it could happen in a heartbeat to any of us.

Since then, MS has continued to take its toll on my mobility. I am able to walk less and less each year… and I can't focus or multi-task like I used to. I struggle with accepting this version of myself. It seems that each week brings some loss and a new adjustment. Life with MS is definitely not simple.

Still, I feel that I'm a fortunate man with MS, in fact, that's the name of my blog. It's helpful to share my thoughts about this new life I've been handed – the good things and the bad things.

On the good side, MS hadn't yet affected my life when my children were young and needed chasing. and then, while I was still working in Washington D.C., I reconnected with and married an old friend from junior high school in Bellevue. She is the kindest and wisest life partner I could ever hope to have. Together, we are part of a community of friends and family who love and support us.

I am also fortunate because my short career provided me with excellent health insurance… generous long term disability insurance… and a stable financial position. MS has also spared most of my cognitive functions – at least so far. I continue to consult at my D.C. law firm… to write and to teach young lawyers… and to be actively engaged with the national MS society.

Finally, I am fortunate because I have hope. You and your support for the national MS society give me hope.

Just look at what society-funded research has already been able to accomplish in the past two decades. There was not one single medication to treat relapsing-remitting MS when I was diagnosed in 1994. Now, thanks to research, there are a dozen approved drugs.

Today, more and more research is being focused on the most progressive forms of the disease… with the hope that one day, scientists will be able to do for progressive MS what they've done for relapsing-remitting – slowing or stopping exacerbations and limiting progression.

But even more exciting for me, the society's research also is investigating how to actually repair function that has already been lost. I truly believe that it is simply a matter of time – and of money – before I will walk again, cane and wheelchair free. And then, the next logical discovery will be a way to end MS forever.

For so many people in our chapter community, hope is also an education made possible by a society scholarship… or a grant to buy an air conditioner… or classes to help them learn to live their best lives with MS. You make all these things possible.

You give the gift of hope to everyone living with MS.

Life with MS is a dance – for me, my wife and everyone we love. Sometimes, MS takes the lead and we must follow. At other times, MS must follow our lead. And sometimes, we even dance ahead of MS… leaving it sitting at the side of the ballroom.

So many people who have less than I do would never have the chance to take the lead in that dance if it were not for the national MS society's resources and support… if it were not for people like you who are here tonight.

Right now, each of you has the opportunity to take the lead

in this dance. Life with MS is not simple. but it is simple for you to make a profound difference for all of us who live with this disease. So please, give generously... and then we will dance."

When You Are "Certain," Think Again, and Then Laugh!

My wonderful aunt who had a place in Maine sent this to me. It says so much about how ridiculous it is to think we are really "certain" of anything.

Actual October 1995 radio transmission between a US Navy vessel and Canadian authorities:

Canadians: Please divert your course 15 degrees south to avoid collision.

US Navy: Recommend YOU divert your course 15 degreesnorth to avoid collision.

Canadians: Negative. Please divert your course 15 degrees south to avoid collision.

US Navy: This is the captain of a US Navy ship. I say again, divert YOUR course. . . . This is the USS Lincoln and we are accompanied by three destroyers, three cruisers, and various support vessels. I DEMAND that you change your course 15 degrees north. Otherwise, countermeasures will be taken to ensure the safety of this ship and its crew.

Canadians: Sir. This is a lighthouse. Your call.

Taken from a "Discover Maine" magazine, 2015.

I felt a surge of anger, sadness, and frustration as she said this to me...

The circumstances of any health condition could give rise to the situation described below. In hindsight, I wish I had asked some more general questions and followed up, but I am also terrified and dismayed by the failure of the medical professionals to ask the question I was not asking.

Spasticity is an important symptom of multiple sclerosis. Based on my latest conversation with a medical professional about this subject, my working understanding of spasticity now includes what has been going on in my weak left leg for the last decade.

Prior to my recent appointment, it had not included my weak left leg, the source of many of my biggest challenges, frustrations, and sadness relating to multiple sclerosis.

Notwithstanding all the images of frozen limbs I looked at for this post, prior to my recent appointment, when I thought of spasticity, I thought of other people experiencing painful cramping and involuntarily jerking of limbs and other body parts.

And yes, my own legs do jerk in the morning and I did know that that is something like spasticity, but I wouldn't come to the conclusion that I actually "had spasticity" or give a yes when asked the question by one of my doctors whether I "was experiencing spasticity." I would never have sought treatment through drugs, for example, for the morning jumping of my legs. Spasticity didn't keep me up at night. Spasticity didn't hurt me. Spasticity didn't seem to be a big deal. It didn't seem to affect my difficulty walking.

Fast forward to my recent appointment. I went to see a physical therapist who is also a specialist in multiple sclerosis. I went to see her because my left knee is having some issues, which although they haven't presented yet in pain are presenting an alarming locking backwards of the knee and troubling stiffness around the knee after it is challenged by, for example, walking up the hill for a while.

It is important here to mention that I took the initiative to make this appointment totally on my own, not because my neurologist had directed me to do it or asked questions that would've drawn out the need to do it.

Through the last 10 years there have been other moments like this one where I did not make appointments with physical therapists because of my schedule, travel, or other interfering factors. But on this day, I did go to see her.

I also went to see her with a much more generalized question about my left leg than I have ever presented to a physical therapist before, even though most of my conversations with physical therapist have had to do with specific issues relating to my left leg. Does that difference in presentation to physical therapists sound like legal hairsplitting to anyone? Does it sound like the old maxim that you only get answers to the questions you actually ask? At this point it does to me!

I had met with this physical therapist before to discuss a custom ankle foot orthotic. This time, with a more generalized presentation, she took the time to examine my knee and quickly came away with the conclusion that my inability to use my left hamstring was not weakness per se but in fact spasticity inside the muscles of the leg that were refusing to budge any higher. She confirmed this by having me sit down facing forward and doing some tests on involuntary shaking of the left foot. She said that what I was experiencing was spasticity in my left leg and that I could very likely be helped by some of the drugs that are taken to lessen the effects of spasticity.

I felt a surge of anger, sadness, and frustration as she said this to me. It was overwhelming. How could I have missed this for so long? How could I have gone without medication that might indeed help me a lot with one of my biggest problems which is my left leg? Did this mean that I was headed for the more serious and painful type of spasticity? On the last point, she reassured me, stating that a diagnosis of spasticity does not necessarily translate into a sentence of greater spasticity. I was comforted but still pretty angry at myself and frankly at my neurologists and at her and my other physical therapists who had worked on my left leg.

For the record I adore my neurologists and think they are some of the best angels in the outfield helping those of us living with multiple sclerosis. For the record, I think my physical therapists have been highly competent and they have asked all the specific questions that I presented to them.

For the record, I'm relatively fond of myself though I do think that I miss things through being too much in my own experience and worried about whatever problem is coming up next without taking the time to widen the frame and look at what is going on in the disease for other people.

That said, if anyone has the ability to widen their frame relating to the disease, you would think someone like me, who is writing a blog about his life with MS, who is an active participant with the national multiple sclerosis society, and who reads about and speaks about issues related to MS, would be someone who might be able to make the connection between the general concept of the word "spasticity" and the chronic devastating weakness of his own left leg

But like I said at the beginning, this could happen to anybody. From now on, I am going to ask general questions about what might be causing everything happening to me and see if there is anything else that might help.

And I am going to be very hopeful about baclofen, the drug my neurologist prescribed. If it helps at all, it will be very sweet, far more sweet than the bitter, the very bitter, of what might have been over the last many years.

When illusion ends, what rushes in? Terror, then hopefully the calming sea.

The MRI showed two new lesions on my brain. My grand illusion evaporated. This illusion, a sturdy structure of columns and marble and rationalization and denial. Gone.

For almost ten years, I had convinced myself that in 2006 the powerful, dangerous drug Tysabri had stopped new lesion growth, this notwithstanding the steady decline in my walking and worsening cognitive issue. Having been ordered by my doctor to move off Tysabri and onto an oral drug in 2012, I dealt with the worry of losing Tysabri by adding to the story that I now had "secondary progressive MS," which meant to me that my slow decline would continue but that no new visible lesions would form.

Not so. There they were, a couple weeks ago, looking at me like two owl eyes from my frontal lobe, the place where executive function lives.

It's terrifying. For so long I have trudged through very complicated chapters – divorce, disability, alienation from children, relocation, progression – thinking I knew something about what the distant shore of new life would hold. Now I don't know. The next lesion or, as always, some invisible white matter damage, could catapult me into a totally different place. Pain, paralysis, optical neuritis, all seem more possible now.

My doctor's immediate response was to try to put me back on Tysabri, but my blood is not ready to receive it without an unreasonable risk of a potentially fatal infection. Maybe in a while it will be ready, but not now. For now, I live with MS but without a disease modifying therapy. The oral medication was an illusion. Maybe Tysabri's efficacy for ten years was an illusion as well.

We all live in a world of illusions, all around us and in our minds. We sometimes call them "working understandings." They are based on some facts, some experience, and often some hope. Some serve us for years and drive many good decisions.

What is not an illusion is that everyone is unique, everyone, and certainly the presentation of the mystery of MS in each person living with MS is unique. We just don't know for sure what will help. All we have are studies with good or great or poor outcomes. All we have is our own experience. The categories of the disease are not linear – some whose MS seems more like "secondary progressive" still have new lesions. Like me now.

And uncertainty is really all we ever have. Things happen. We try to get the best information and counsel we can, but ultimately, we must make a decision about what to do, every day.

So, I now must become bigger, become a wave that is part of a vast ocean. I must let the tide take over, and if a good option arises again, hurl myself upon it. Until then, you will find me tying to float on the water of faith, faith that the universe unfolds as intended. I have struggled my whole life to find this faith, to feel the supportive water beneath me. looks like time to cast off....

Fifty Shades of GREEN-man

Nothing physical has really changed. The state of being, however, has moved slowly, creeping from a brave hunter green and then bleeding out, oozing and settling into a sickening swamp till a few days ago.

Words are two dimensional and imperfect, but they are all I have to communicate what is happening. Belief and faith are three dimensional, like the water under the body as we float or falter, thrashing and gasping to fill our lungs with the divine air of life. Told in words, this is the story of how my faith grew since my last post. My angels — family, friends, colleagues, support team, et al. — in person and texts and emails and books have showered me with loving words and touch.

Springing from this are the words below. They all carried me here to a place where I haltingly declare and dare this stupid disease to progress, because as God is my witness, I almost truly believe.

Here are the words, often repeated, from these last weeks —

"You are a person. Not a rock or a tree. You received the gift of conscious life. This moment is part of your life. This moment is terrifying. Moments can be terrifying or beautiful or both. Trust that it is important to be with what is. Hold the terror and dark. It is an inescapable part of the human experience. Allow it a place. Hold along with it your history of strength. Fill up on your journey to this point and become bigger and bigger. All you have done. All you have suffered. All of it. All the laughter and tears and joy and failures. Every tree, mountain, and breeze. All. Now hold all those moments of everyone you love and who loves you. If you can, hold all the worlds' too.

You are big. You are rich in the stuff of this human life. You received all this as a member in a group of humans living here at this time. They made you, you. Beautiful you. Believe they will continue to make you more. Not less. They cannot take what you have already done. They cannot make you unworthy of the kind of love that matters in this weary wonderful world. Believe. It may take time to believe. You may have far to go for this.

We all still work on it. It begins with today. This hour. With breathing. Breathe. Dismiss negative self-talk like feathers of nothing. Move toward loving what is now. A job done with love. A walk if you can. A dog. A stretch. A hug. Always, a breath. And the three dimensions of lungs filling. And putting the air in the blood to be carried on sacred paths to all parts of the miracle body. Patience as the days pass in darkness. Do not despair. Breathe and be as present as the murk allows. Forgiving yourself for being stuck. Rest. Work. Listen to music. Cry. Talk to those you love.

And after many days of this, holding the darkness, one day people will seem beautiful again. The swamp lightens and you begin to lift. And your internal music turns. From a dirge or the blues, to some reggae and then pumping dance music . . . ooonce!! ooonce!! ooonce!!

The sun is shining. It always was. This work of believing that we will be loved and continue honorably even if we must sometimes hold the dark, is a majestic, gritty, magical road of every human life. We hope to give this belief to our children. But they are not our children. They are the sons and the daughters of life longing for itself. They must build it themselves.

Had I not doubted so in chapters past, I would have believed more and sooner. And whatever happened, I would have been sturdier and more present.

True belief always surpasses fear. So please, do what you need to do to believe — that you are worthy and that the universe is unfolding as it was meant to unfold for your unique story on this small rock close to a lesser sun.

Surely if you believe, a beautiful moment or journey or person waits for you somewhere. hold the dark and be patient."

For me today, the shade of green is from a comic book. I have obtained a set of t-shirts for my workouts, each representing a different superhero. Today, I put on the t-shirt of the Green Lantern. It's sparkling, radiant green almost requiring sunglasses. That's where you find me today, more ready than before, hopeful and more certain that whatever happens will not take away who I am.

c'mon future.! I dare you!

A Little Stress Relief

My blood is not ready to receive the powerful drug Tysabri
yet, so I am still exposed to a disease whose progression
continues. But, in the meantime, I have found a stress
reliever at the free puppy play school at my local
Petco. Anne Romney may have her horses. This is what I
have, ever the fortunate man.

It happened on a grimy New York subway in 1985

I wasn't prepared. I was not prepared at all for how loud the subway was, how dirty it was, and how it shook as if it would fall right off the tracks. It smelled and was covered with graffiti. My first New York subway ride was in 1985, with a new friend in the tender first week of college. It brought a moment that will stay with me forever.

The black man near me on the subway was enormous. He had the biggest arms I have ever seen in person. He sat calmly as we rattled along, and when we reached our stop, he followed us closely.

He followed us in his wheelchair, with his huge arms and his Vietnam fatigues. He had no legs. He followed us and shortly outpaced us, arriving at the bottom of a long, long flight of stairs.

This was New York before clean subways. Ronald Reagan was president. Ed Koch was mayor. John Gotti was about to have his men gun down Paul Castellano at Sparks steakhouse. And I was about to encounter the strongest man I've ever met in a moment that would probably not happen today, in the land of ADA accommodations, blade runners, electric wheelchairs, and plentiful elevators.

 At the bottom of the grimy, oily stairs, he turned to me and said "could you get my chair?" Before I even had a chance to say yes, he somehow swung his body and planted his hands on the filthy cement.

As we looked on in amazement, he swung his torso up each stair, following with his arms and then up the next stair and the next stair and the next. I had to run with the wheelchair to keep up with him. When I reached the top, he climbed back into his chair, said thanks, and rolled away, leaving us open mouthed, watching him move down the dark sidewalk.

The story of meeting the Vietnam veteran in his chair in my first week of college foreshadowed my story and has taken on new meaning as my legs have slowly weakened. I think again and again of him swinging himself up those awful stairs. Why did I find myself getting off at the same subway stop near anyone so remarkable? Was he real? Did it really happen? As I struggle to keep up my strength and composure, how can I ever approach despair in the face of this memory?

 The answers to these questions are the stuff of this ongoing journey. I do know one thing for certain. No matter how strong, we all come to places where we need help to move on. There are many, most known and some strangers, who carry my figurative chair up the stairs when I get to a place where I feel like I can't possibly go further. My strong and beautiful wife, my family, my friends, my wonderful law firm, my partners at the MS Society, and all of you who react to these words are carrying something with me. You notice, listen, wonder, encourage and nourish (with turkey today).

Without you, I would be sitting at the bottom of those stairs in a dark place full of noise and danger. Because of you, I am lifted up and can bump forward on this journey. We will soldier on. I am so very grateful that you have been at these various subway stops with me. Thank you. Today, and every day.

 Happy Thanksgiving.

The Ribs that Saved Christmas: How I Broke Five Ribs and Learned the Holiday's True Meaning

On the fifth day of Christmas

My true life gave to me

FIVE BROKEN RIBS

Four firemen

Three helpful friends

Two barking dogs

And a comedian as an EMT.

On the evening of Friday, December 4, I fell and broke five

ribs. This is the story of my ribs and how I am now happier than I have been in a long time. I am not a Pollyanna. Anyone who knows me or who has read this entire blog can attest to that. I have not talked myself into these positive feelings. They just happened, at a level way below my demanding, fickle, restless mind. Almost as soon as I fell, I felt strongly a calm and a joy and a sense of love and belonging.

And I can't seem to explain why. So, to borrow from the sage they called Seuss:

"It could be, perhaps, that his shoes were too tight.

It could be his head wasn't screwed on just right.

But I think that the most likely reason of all

May have been that his heart was two sizes too small."

 It could be my walls need some grab bars just right.

Or I need a cool walker for walking at night.

But whatever the reason, grab bar or the walls,

My ribs have brought things not expected at all.

They brought good news that

The fall did not puncture a lung.

No head bleed. No back crack. No bell getting rung.

 And then more than each of these obvious things,

I learned that my pain has no legs and no wings

I found that my friends rallied right in real time.

I learned once again — life can change on a dime,

and those old dragging problems now seem really just fine.

So, sit back and let me tell you the story of the ribs before

Christmas:

T'was some nights before Christmas

And all through the house

Not a creature was stirring

Not even a mouse

Or a 15-year-old stepson

Or a kind big brother visiting from Dallas

And I in my t-shirt and mom

With a dog on her lap

Were just settling down for a short winter's nap

When at the side of our bed

There arose such a clatter that Jack and Sam rushed in the room to see what was the matter.

On my way from the bathroom to our own tender bed,

My left leg had buckled.

I rolled, saving my head

and landed with all of my weight right on the tip top

of a fan sitting up on a big wooden block.

 Broke five ribs,

One dangling like a snapped branch almost ready to fall.

In six weeks I can laugh, burp, cough, hiccup and all.

But right now, I live after "the night of the ribs"

And I've found that it brings something more than pain meds. For years I've worked with my trainers to strengthen my core

My stomach and abs, with my feet on the floor

Aimed at balance and posture

Like old yogis of yore.

But despite daily practice and trying real hard

My head could not stop talking and thinking out loud

I frustrate and berate me as again I would fail

Till "Rib Friday" which hit on the head of the nail

No broke arm, no split head, no sprain would suffice

My gut had to get hit, ribs caught in a vice

And not just one rib or two rib, only five ribs would do

So I can sit here and tell this cool story to you.

It's as if my body took over and courageously said,

"If you can't come to ground and get out of your head,

then I'll do it for you in my own way instead."

So like old Scrooge in that tale from so long ago

My ghosts came in one night

Firemen, doctors, techs in one go

All gave me a big fright.

But that last ghost, "tech x-ray"

He really topped them all.

Shoved me this way and that way

Worse pain than the fall.

Still, they got me together

And helped focus my soul

On what's really important

Finally near that old goal

So they heard me exclaim

As Lisa drove home out of sight

"Thanks for reaching my center (finally)

And to all a good night!"

 Wishing everyone holidays full of joy, health, and presence.

<u>**2016**</u>

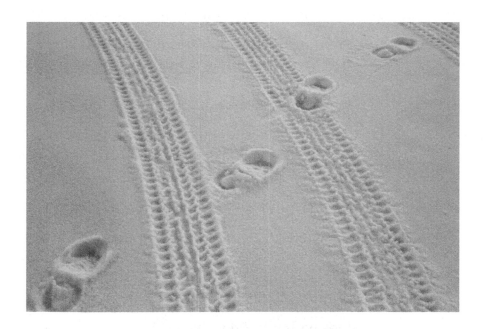

It's time. time for the hardest part. So let's roll.

This post is the one I have feared since the blog began.

Turning it over and over, wondering what it would be like, when it would arrive. It's time now.

May bravery mark my rolling over this most dreaded threshold, because true "stepping over" can no longer happen. It's time now. I've tried so hard. But now it's time.

From now on, when I head out, I will be in an electric wheelchair or on a scooter. I will use a walker to make my way gingerly around the house and see how long that lasts

This moment has come in slowly and on its own time. strewn with the burning wrecks of walking a little bit better one day or barking at my loving wife for some stupid trifle another day, it loomed and heaved like big waves on the ocean. Far off shore and then suddenly upon me, the waves never relented. Until today.

A month ago, no one would have identified me as being "in a wheelchair." Using one at airports and on long walks during vacations did not qualify. In conversation, I would report losing half my walking ability each year. I could manage some steps with my stylish canes. I spoke of trying to plateau with my private workouts.

No more. It's over. My recent, brief flirtation with the much better stability of European crutches (a bit like the old polio crutches) failed to suffice due to neuropathy, the same issue that ultimately doomed the cane. After about 50 agonizingly slow yards at most, my legs and energy vanish, leaving me near falling and drained for hours. I can still use the crutches for short hops. But it's time.

It's time to start researching the best devices and improvements for this stage where, thank God, I can still transfer from walker to chair to bed to bathroom, and where my right leg still works well enough to get me slowly up the stairs in our house.

It's time to wrap my mind around the image of the wheelchair versus the cane. Having read a lot and spoken to those who know, the news is not great. You get shorter. Some say you disappear. No one else is at eye level; they all stand above your gaze.

You resent people not sitting with you: "how can they not see that I am down here?" Cocktail parties bring a toxic mix of anger and sadness. Unless you buy an expensive elevated chair, you won't ever stand eye to eye with anyone again.

It's time to heed the wise advice of the occupational

therapist: focus on getting to destinations by the easiest route and conserving energy, rather than walking for its own sake.

It's time. Time because ignoring what time it is now would be to risk the kind of fall I had last month, when I broke five ribs. My sister-in-law Claire, a physician, told me and Lisa that it can certainly be too late to go to the chair. Then she asked kindly, "can it ever be too soon?"

It's time to gently tell my friends and loved ones that for now, I need to focus on inhabiting this transition. I do understand that research is advancing and that I could someday improve. But in order to move forward without a repeat of the violent lurching between hope and fear that marked 2015, I must live inside today, tomorrow, and the next day. The long term will take care of itself.

It's time to move past my longstanding fear of this moment and past some charming recent additions. Adding insult to injury, new leg spasms have arrived, as if to punctuate my decline in walking. They attack when I attempt to stand up after sitting a bit, shaking my body uncontrollably and catapulting me backward into my seat or my bed. As I move through the fear of the wheelchair and toward acceptance of the spasms, I hope I can cut down on the crying. Did you ever notice that lots and lots of tears taste like a perfectly chlorinated pool on a summer day when you were young? I fall to sobbing when a song or an image presents an opportunity to release more of my seemingly endless tears. This grief will run its course, slow or fast, long or less long.

It's time to join ranks with more seasoned cavalry officers–the ones with years in the saddle. I will look to them for wisdom and comfort. I know I will find some there.

Most of all, it's time to draw strength from the clarity; the threshold has finally been crossed. It has happened. It. Is. Time.

I will see you on the other side, and if you see a twinkle in my eye or hear a lilt in my voice, please laugh with me. On other days, please tell me you are sorry that this is where I am right now. I will tell you that it is okay. And it is.

Let's roll.

The First Day with My New Electric Wheelchair

It was fitting that my first destination with my new electric wheelchair was the annual morning retreat of the board of the NW Chapter of the National MS Society. As Lisa and I had hoped when we saw it at the store, the chair is indeed very unobtrusive, more like a chair on wheels. It also sits me taller than I had anticipated. It comes apart fairly easily, and the first outing was a great success.

A Sign for a Broken Road

Happy when it appeared, I parked with glee.

Walking up the steps, but knowing the sign meant more

than parking.

Rolling down the hill to where the image there

was me now bumping across the change.

With tags and stickers teenagers' and anarchists' deco

The change it is not clean.

Discouraged, trying to be brave

we all roll to our fate.

Good days and those other days, we ride the broken road.

The sign, with tags, it cheers us on.

Walk/Run MS is approaching. The GREEN MANiacs are gathering...

Last year, the GREEN MANiacs made a big splash at the Walk MS event. We are hoping for an even bigger team this year on April 10. Participation and not size of donation is our goal. (We will also have nifty new t-shirts.)

Please join the team.

Guess what came out of the mud?

I have arrived. I am home. I have arrived. I am home.

These are the words of a powerful meditation described by the legendary Thich Nhat Hahn, Vietnamese Buddhist leader and author. Of his many books, I found these in *"No Mud, No Lotus."*

No kidding.

There's been a lot of mud described here in the last few posts, so I thought I'd describe a Lotus that bloomed in Washington DC recently.

I have arrived. I am home.

These are the words now blooming deep inside my heart

after my visit to DC, lifted up by the support of my wonderful work family for the past 20 years.

Home is where family is. Home is where people care about your happiness, and you care about theirs. Home is a place where you feel like you matter.

Fortunate to have a warm, loving home in Seattle, I returned after several months working remotely to the presence of my old colleagues and my Virginia friends and family. Fundraising for the Run/Walk MS event in April, I had tossed out an email to the firm. Within a couple of days, almost $19,000 rolled in — donations from partners to secretaries — people at every level of the organization. Within a week, the total was over $34,000. And while counting money as a measure of anything is always dangerous and imperfect, I feel like there was a message. In fact the message was actually said and sent in words, time and time again.

I have arrived. I am home.

That powerful meditation described by Thich Nhat Hahn was a walking meditation. Mine won't always be walking, but it is powerful just the same.

Inspiration on a Newark New Jersey flight to DC

It had not been a good travel day, filled with a familiar mix of sadness and worry. The dumps are not good traveling companions when you live with multiple sclerosis.

 As I hobbled slowly down the jetway to my flight, a soft force from behind asked if I needed anything. Giving my usual response of "no thanks, I'm just slow," I turned to see the sturdy young woman I had heard asking about pre-boarding for military even as she made way for me at the top of the ramp. I said "thank you for your service." She smiled and continued on.

Boarding the plane always presents a big challenge because

of the need for speed. As I made my way slowly down the aisle of the small jet, she approached and asked if she could take my crutches. She tried unsuccessfully to fit them in the overhead, resorting with my consent to adjusting their length.

When we landed, I waited in my seat as usual so as not to hold up deplaning while I embark on yet another rolling airport adventure. I noticed that the soldier was waiting also, and as soon as the last passenger went by, she came over to readjust my crutches and hand me my bag. A bit overwhelmed, I asked about her branch of service, and she said she was a marine. "of course you are," said I, to which she replied–"it's not because I am a marine. it's what my mother taught me."

Kind assistance lights my way, especially in my home and office, with friends and around the neighborhood. For some reason, her kindness that day shone with particular honor and good timing. Sempre fi, and thanks very much to the teaching of a mother from Birmingham, Alabama.

The Spirit Award, May 14, 2016

Photo by Step-son, Sam Vila

On May 14, 2016 in Seattle, my law partner and friend Dane presented me with the 2016 Spirit Award of the Northwest Chapter of the National Multiple Sclerosis Society. We had 12 partners and many other friends and family who flew a long way for a weekend in Seattle. Our friends, colleagues, and family totaled 70 people. We raised over $1.2 million from 350 attendees.

It was one of the best days of my life. As always, I thank everyone for their wonderful support.

Here is the transcription of the introduction by Dane Butswinkas and my speech.

Please welcome Dane Butswinkas to the stage here with us tonight from the other Washington, the one with DC after it from the law firm of Williams and
Connolly.

Dane

Emerson wrote: *the only person you're destined to become is the person that you decide to be.*

Gil Greenman decided long ago. He decided to be courageous, inspirational, heroic.

Terms that have become almost cliche and reserved for our sports legends and our music greats. But I have the honor tonight to introduce you to a real rock star.

I have known Gil Greenman since 1996. The Columbia University scholar, the Harvard Law School graduate. The accomplished litigator and trial Lawyer. The author, the mentor to young lawyers at my law firm in Washington D.C. The guy who was smart enough to do his judicial clerkship in Honolulu. My colleague, my law partner and my friend.

But I want to spend a few minutes talking to you not about Gil Greenman the Lawyer but about Gil Greenman the person.

<u>Resilience!</u>

A lot of people made submissions on Gil's behalf and I read them. Everyone without exception had a friend, a colleague or a family member recounting private personal interactions with Gil showing his remarkable resilience. Each anecdote showed a confrontation with a struggle, a disappointment, an obstacle. And every one of the anecdotes ended the same way. A person who picked himself up and dusted himself off and moved forward with a kind of optimism that can't help but be contagious.

A person who refused to be defined by multiple sclerosis. A person who was making triumphs small but meaningful

every day against the disease. A person who lived by the old
Japanese proverb: fall down seven times stand up eight.

Inspiration!

So how does Gil Greenman pick himself up?
Well, Booker T Washington said: *if you*
want to lift yourself up lift up others.

That's what Gil does on a daily basis: whether it's mentoring
people with multiple sclerosis or giving litigator tips to his
stepson Sam before a big speech last year or counseling the
young lawyers at our firm in Washington DC, Gil has
inspired all of those around him.

It was not surprising to see in one of the submissions for
someone to write, and I quote: *to know Gil and be around Gil*
makes it impossible not to want to be a better
Person.

Dignity!

Above all Gil does everything with honesty, decency and

dignity. He is a role model to all of us. He has taught us that the quietest voice can have the loudest impact,

that time is precious and stingy don't waste it, and that the measure of how you leadpeople is not through the steps that you take. He is living proof that Emerson was Right.

But we're not going to let Gil off easy. He has a lot more work to do, a lot more blogs, a lot more articles, a lot more talks, a lot more parenting, a lot more people to inspire, a lot more life to live.

Gil battles the daily fights with multiple sclerosis because he knows as do his friends, his friend's families and his family and colleagues know that he has a lot of unfinished business a lot more to contribute. I would turn maybe to someone from Massachusetts since that's where Gil is from and since we have a 1920 scene to Babe Ruth the former Boston Red Sox slugger in the 20s. I know it's a sore spot Gil, even, even a hundred years later but when confronted with the challenge of strikeouts Babe Ruth was quoted as saying: every strike gets me closer to my next home run.

My dad was a naval officer and he had a term that he would

describe Gil's accomplishments with. It was a term that he reserved for those special accomplishments that were the best of the best. It was called Bravo Zulu. It means job well done and he certainly would think that it applies to Gil. It is my great pleasure and in fact my honor to introduce you to the 2016 Spirit Award Winner Gil Greenman.
[Applause]

Gil:

Gonna get ready here - (takes out handkerchief)
These trial lawyers, you know it's one of the best trial lawyers in the country that you just heard. We have several other very notable lawyers from Williams and Connolly here and all of them, all 12 partners who flew out here for a weekend in Seattle can you believe that 12 Williams and Conolly partners here for me, this day, in Seattle.
You almost kind of want to do a Sally Field and say: *they like me they really like me*
But what I wanted to talk about was the fact that I have this out (handkerchief) for a reason.
People ask me sometimes when they see the progression happening and you saw me, many of you, speak last year I was here doing the ask. I had a cane. Walking with a cane

but getting around pretty well and now it's a year later and it's dramatically, dramatically different and you know the progression is happening and that's just a fact of life. That is what's going on and people ask me how do you cope with this and how do you do some of the things that Dane said and even some of the ones I actually did not the ones you talked about but yes some of the ones Dane said how do you face some of this? how do you get this resilience? One really good way is crying. I cry, I cry all the time. I cry at baseball games. I cry. I cry watching shows that aren't even sad. I'll cry, I'll cry for no reason whatsoever. In fact, one time I was watching the Christmas Carol with my kids and for some reason Marley's ghost really got to me and I just started bawling my eyes out and crying and crying and crying, like uncontrollably crying because I had, I like to say I have ten thousand tears inside and I need to just get them out, so when I get the opportunity I'll just go ahead and cry you know you should all do that really. But I do it for sure and and so some of my ten thousand are coming out and Sam, my stepson, looks over at me and I said: 'what'? and he says: it's the Muppets, Muppets Christmas Carol.

Let me say okay. So before I get really going here I want to pause and do one thing which is to dedicate this award with all my heart to the most powerful angel that I know.

The person who walks this journey with me every day and if you know anyone with MS who's partnered they will tell you that their partner also has MS so Congratulations she has chosen to do that out of her own free will which I often question but she is the love of my life the beautiful Dr. Lisa Hebner Villa and I want to dedicate this award to her. Thank you, my love, for making this life possible. Without her I would not be standing here I don't really think I'd probably even be alive.

Now I want to tell you a story about resilience and about the way MS affects life. You gotta watch out because it's, it's, I don't know it's one of those stories. It's a lawyer story, sorry. So I'm a second year associate at this incredible law firm that I was so lucky to get a job at. I was just so excited and then in my second year unbelievably a case involving organized crime lands in my lap like we're gonna go talk about the mafia and the facts of this case were like something out of a Grisham novel or a movie I mean I could, I could go on and on if it wasn't confidential about everything that happened. But just trust me it was one of those cases and it boiled down to basically you know; their guy was a bad guy and said that our guy was a bad guy and we said no he's not a bad guy and we had to prove that he wasn't a bad guy. So that was what it was and to do that we had to cross-examine FBI protected witnesses who were in the witness protection program.

I'm a second-year lawyer and you know, a lot of law is frankly really boring, a lot of banking law and stuff like that and we have to do that to get the bills paid but this case was about the mafia. This case was about somebody who actually you see on tv and you'd worry about it and you think wow protected witness this is so exciting! Needless to say, I was very excited about this case

The first witness gets on the stand and I'll just give one away one fact. This guy's name was Nino Cuccinada. I am not making this up. I'm not making this up, that's all I can say though.

He has a nervous breakdown on the stand. Literally he's telling the story about how he went to prison because somebody disrespected him in a bar and he went and put one in the guy's forehead and then threw the gun into the water and then went home and waited for his daughter to call the cops. He is the most pathetic mobster I've ever seen and not a smart one either but he was their witness. So he was breaking apart on the stand when the prosecutors were calling we're asking him questions and we're thinking what do we do about this?

Now most Williams and Connolly lawyers and the partner I was working for in that case in particular have one approach with a witness whose credibility is on the line which is to kill them. The lawyer, the partner who I was with, who's not here tonight, wanted to take this witness down and just take him apart. Now I'm a second-year guy and he's asked me what my advice is. I say you know I think the guy already kind of took himself apart. I think we should talk to him kind of like he's a mental patient. You know we could really be really careful with him show him documents and kind of creep away you know. The other thing that the witness had done is that he saw the mafia everywhere. He said that you know the dog catcher's mobbed, up the banker is mobbed up, the mayor is mobbed up, the congressman's mobbed up. Actually I think the mayor actually was mobbed up but everybody else is mobbed up. He saw the mob everywhere. The partner says to me what should we say about that? We

have to sum that up in like a one-liner. My favorite thing
to do in my legal career was to come up with one-liners. So I
thought for a minute and I said: ask him if it's ever been said
of him if he looks at the world through mob colored glasses.
The partner loved this and so I'm just that night I'm just so
excited this is my first big trial I'm a second year associate.
I've got my job. I got everything I wanted I've worked my
whole life for this.

I'm at the courthouse the first day and the morning the
second day of trial. The partner and the client are going to be
there in 20 minutes. I'm with the advanced team. I'm
standing in the lobby of this beautiful courthouse in my
Brooks Brothers blue suit and I'm ready to go and I'm so
earnest and so eager and then MS enters in. No one at the
firm knew that I had MS at that time. I hadn't heard that
much from the disease since my diagnosis my third
year in law school but it showed up. One of the things that
MS does is that it messes with your bowels. So standing in
the lobby of that courthouse on that wonderful day, the
second day of my trial of my first violent legal career,
everything I'd eaten for the last three days came right out of
the back of me. Can you imagine? Standing there in this

crowded courthouse lobby and I'm just completely dumbfounded and the stress! I mean like this is my career, this is my life, my life is over. Over. It reminded me of another little story so I'm going to put that Gil over here and actually I'm putting me further over there because you know that's just happened.

A nine-year-old version of me who had followed a friend out on some ice on a frozen river in West Virginia, a river that had never frozen ever before ever. I'm out on this ice and all of a sudden this guy on a freeway overpass stops in traffic, no median, gets out of his car and says: you damn kids get off that river and we suddenly realize that we're going to die because we're too close to the middle of the river and that's a very fast flowing dangerous river and so I'll never forget.

Looking at my poor brother who did not come out on the river and was waiting for us to come back and walking those 50 paces to the side of the bank, you could hear the ice. You feel the ice crunching under your feet and the river rushing you just knew it and the reason I'm telling you this story and the other story is because I believe in angels. I believe the reason that I'm anywhere near anything that Dane described to you is because of angels.

I already introduced you to the most powerful angel, my wife, but there were unseen angels that day in West Virginia and the water the ice did not crack did not break down I did not fall into that river which is the reason I'm standing here today.

And then standing in that courthouse I looked out and I saw a taxicab 50 yards away. I made my way out somehow to the most unlucky taxi cab driver in the history of taxi cab drivers. I threw $200 at him and I said please, please take me to my hotel. Thank God he didn't throw me out of his cab. So he took me there and then I see that I'm gonna have to walk to the side door the hotel where I know any moment the partner and the client are going to come out, any moment. And again, it's like the ice in the river. 50 paces. 50 paces what's going to happen, what's going to happen?
And they didn't come out. They didn't come out. I believe it's because they're angels. I think the angels exist. I wanted to talk about those unseen angels and a little story about how MS affected my life early in my early career.

The angels that are here now tonight are the angels of the MS society who put on this event and do such incredible work to raise funds for research to cure this terrible disease. They're angels all of them, and most of them are women so it's sort of easy to say they're all angels and picture them that way. At this and at the society most of the employees are women but they've become my family, my family. And so I want I call them angels. Then the angels of my whole family are here. My actual family have flown in from all over the country to be here my father, my mother, my brother and sister-in-law, everyone is here. My Aunt and her wife from Massachusetts . My son is here. My step-kids are here and My in-laws Patty and Larry. Larry has become my sherpa who pushes me all over New York City in a wheelchair. I mean unbelievable these people they're, angels they're angels, I tell you they are, they are.

Then again 12 partners from Williams and Connelly flew across the country to be here today. I will never ever get over that I still can't quite believe it. I'm so grateful and they are my angels. And last our dear friends. Lisa and I have the most amazing community of friends here who are so supportive and so, so loving and so caring and so without all

111

these angels you don't get this kind of spirit so the spirit is not just me it's from them and all of you really so I just want to say thank you!

Then I want to close this little speech by talking directly to multiple sclerosis for a minute.

We are spiritual beings having a human experience. We're angels, we're spiritual beings having a human experience. My human experience involves multiple sclerosis. So as such a spiritual being I want to address the disease: you stupid, hateful, disease.

Do you not understand that we have thousands and thousands of angels around us?

Do you not understand that if you strike one of us down a thousand more will take their place? You're going to be like polio. You're going to be like polio kids are going to read about you in books and people are going to just not even think about you ever again when this day comes, and it's gonna come, so get your shots in now because by God your days are numbered because our connections,

because the connections of us angels will set us free. Thank you!

[Applause]

Some Good News from an Old Buddy

My left leg sucks, no two ways about it. But last week, it started to suck worse, like a lot worse, like dragging a leg-shaped sack of flour that was also stuck with magnets to the metal ground. When changes like this happen, even to parts of me that are already badly broken, I get anxious and sad. I worry that this is the new normal. I worry that it will never get better again. My good news is that my left leg is back to its usual version of suck instead of the new version of completely and terribly and awfully sucking. It's still the major symptom that impacts my day, this leg that won't cooperate. But at least it is not the ball and chain that crashed into my life for two days last week. Gratitude is something that I try to muster every single day. I have so much to be grateful for. And today, I am with some irony declaring gratitude for "Pokey" – what I long ago started calling my renegade left leg. Thank you, Pokey, for coming back to your standard version of not-so-great. Thank you for not staying where you were last week.

Do I know why Pokey came back? I don't. I don't pretend to understand why things happen sometimes in my neuropathy-plagued system. It may have been increased amounts of coffee in the morning that have given me quite a bit more energy (pursuant to the recent findings of our friends at the World Health Organization). It may have been the workouts that I have tried very hard not to miss for the last two weeks even though there was some heat that came into town and laid me out for a couple days. It may be that on the days that my left leg was bad I rested, other than the workouts. I really have no idea.

What I do know is that even though he sucks, I'm glad to

have Pokey back for now. Ride like the wind Pokey! Or at
the very least ride just a little bit longer. Please.

To Be Known and to Be Loved, a Poem

To be known And to be loved

To be known and loved

Is to walk

To walk a path

Where feet don't touch

But the ground feels verdant green

To be known And to be loved

Is to float

To float

Down a gentle winding river

Which sings secrets in your wake

To be known And to be loved

Is to fly

To fly soaring

With eagles and currents

Diving near ground and then up to clouds again.

Thank you to those

Who have known and loved me

You have made a path where I don't need legs,

A river where I don't need oars, and

An endless blue sky where dreams have come true.

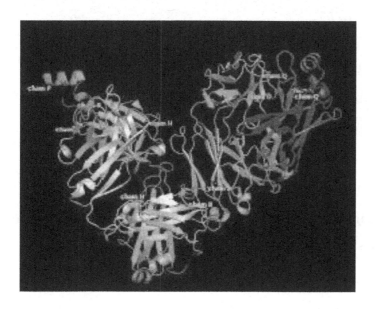

At last, a disease modifying therapy

I'm looking at three doors. I venture through one, and three more appear. Then three more, and three more. The light is dim. The doors are white. White like lab coats. Nothing but white doors.

And then the ticking starts. Tick. Tick. Tick. I can't get it out of my head now. This clock ticking. Doors opening and closing. My anxiety builds. I'm frantic. I am afraid.

Then I wake up. But this is no dream. This is the story of my year-long search for a treatment, a disease-modifying therapy that will halt or at least slow this inexorable disease.

It's gone like this: first, discover last summer new lesions on my frontal lobe while taking the drug Tecfidera. Then wait half the year to go back on Tysabri, the powerful drug that had worked for me before. Next, learn that Tysabri has a one-in-76 chance of killing me. Decide on Rituximab, only to find that insurance won't cover it because it has no formal indication for MS. All the while, my body is failing and the clock is ticking. I am and have been wide open to this disease for almost a year.

But behind another door are the promising new stem cell trials. Doctors are actually using the word "cure" relating to these. But not for me. My neurologist carefully explained that all of the experience from the successful use and Canadian studies points to one conclusion for patients with my presentation: I would go through a traumatic and expensive four-month process, risk my life by having my immune system wiped out and rebuilt, and for all this would almost certainly see no improvement. This is mostly because I have had the disease too long, and in its current state it is now progressing through frequent lesions.

I sat in the doctor's office despondent. They had never seen me so down, prompting the OT to remind me that many people enjoy very fulfilling lives in wheelchairs and urging me to schedule a PT appointment to consider more options for a chair that I could use inside the house. Ashamed, I said I would go, though it was the last thing I wanted to face right now.

Later, the neurologist texted me that she had forgotten to mention another less drastic method with stem cells being done in Chicago. I read the article, and here is what it had to say about the likes of me – those with secondary progressive MS and for more than 10 years. No stem cells for me under current protocols. I missed the stem cell train by just a couple of cars it seems. Adding insult to injury, things were beginning to look like I would have to wait maybe as much as a year for a new drug to guard against further attacks.

Then the next day came the unbelievable news that the insurer had granted my appeal and would in fact pay for Rituximab, the "arthritis" drug which should have been indicated for MS years ago. Like Tysabri, it should protect against new lesions like the ones I learned of last summer. It also may have beneficial effects by calming inflammation.

As I was leaving after my first infusion, I also noticed a talk

being given about drugs that will remyelinate or regrow damaged myelin, presenting the possibly of improvement in symptoms. Onward to six-hour long rituximab infusions, two done for now, two more in six months. With a disease modifying therapy and a dash of long-term hope for improvement, I'll take it.

11:17 am

Sitting at my desk, I can feel them watching me. They lie low and out of my sight which is focused on my computer. But I know that they're watching. I even know what they're thinking. My dogs are thinking "will he ever get up from the chair and go somewhere else so that something interesting might happen." 'No. Not now. Not here and now. '

In this moment I am taking a break from looking at work

emails. I am sitting. I have good energy. I am cooled by a fan sitting a few feet behind me and blowing directly on my back, supplementing our central air-conditioning. Sun streaming in from the windows across the stairs joins the artificial light in the ceiling above me. It's perfectly bright outside, it is a beautiful, sunny but very hot day.

It's 11:17 am.

I was thinking about work until just now when I started thinking about here and now. It's a minute in which I'm not fatigued, not struggling in the bathroom, and not limping along with my walker in the house trying not to fall. Those times are in motion, harder though not impossible to really manage.

Here and now, I feel good. The faces of family smile down on me from the wall where pictures are hung. I am wearing a polo shirt and a pair of shorts and my biomass device on my knee so that when I do walk, I can lift my left toe. I can feel myself breathing and I can almost hear or feel my mind smiling. Honoring the here and now infuses a measure of the sacred. This is where I am. This is who and where I was meant to be. All this from a moment that occurs every day. Really nothing at all. Or, maybe it's everything.

The story no one wants to read

Electric shocks sizzle through her neck, scalp, and face. This is trigeminal neuralgia, sometimes called the "suicide symptom." Occipital neuralgia joins in with brutal migraines. At night, she wakes to spasms like the muscle ripping from the bone. They leave her sobbing. Sometimes she feels like she can barely breathe and other times barely swallow. She has been confined to a wheelchair for several years. Air travel has become too much. She loves quilting but loses the function of her right hand after an hour. Her husband gave up his career as a commercial air pilot in order to take care of her.

People living with MS sometimes find each other on the street. This is how Lisa and I met Debbie and her husband Don in Walla Walla. A conversation about my wheelchair and some emails that followed brought forth from Don exactly what Debbie is going through. These are the kindest people, already offering to put Lisa and me up in their spacious house the next time we are visiting Walla Walla. Just regular folks who once enjoyed a life in the Pacific Northwest, with Don flying and Debbie teaching. All gone now.

Everyone living with MS knows that each story is individual and unique. The picture of the disease that we paint needs to take into account some of the harsher parts. Debbie's story is one. Diagnosed in 2008, Debbie suffered from major relapses and steadily worsened. Some of her symptoms can be managed with medication, but at some point the levels become dangerous and options more limited. Conversations can turn to lines in the sand and endgame strategy.

Many people living with MS suffer from symptoms like Debbie's. We don't often meet them on the street, but they should never be forgotten when we think about what MS is and does.

This is a wicked disease. I spent years avoiding the MS society because I did not want to confront just how bad it can be. When we touch MS — as a person living with it, a partner, a friend, a supporter of the MS society or anyone — we beg the uncomfortable question: "how much do I want to know?" We must make the choice between denial and discomfort. If you have read this far, you may be uncomfortable. But if you are also moved, we win one more little victory over this disease.   People like Debbie are certainly worth the trouble.

An Urban Symphony with Extra Needles

I have an acupuncturist. (hope you do too.) His office
perches high in a stately old downtown structure called the
securities building. It is a 1916 gem, full of the flair of that
age. But like many old buildings, this one has poor
circulation. The peaceful office, tastefully adorned with
Buddhist images and prayer flags, felt like a sauna to me. So
my acupuncturist opened a window in my room.

City sounds immediately washed in, bringing the general

hum of all that is Seattle. After my needles were in, I stared at the ceiling and tried to meditate on my breath. Not today. Frustrated, I smoldered until a set of sounds came together in my conscious mind.

Against the pallet of the city's hum spread soft Zen music from a cd player in the corner. The volume allowed for hearing but not being overwhelmed by the music. Like the city sounds, it was just white noise unless you focused.

As I listened with complete attention, the combination of the music and hum grew into an urban symphony. Squealing brakes ended in long cello notes. Honking horns in sitar chords. Far off voices punctuated pan flutes. The hum joined soft drums, thrumming in the belly of the sounds.

And then, "Damn it. My nose itches. Can't move. OK, OK. Feel the itch. Be the itch." The itch dissipated, and the music returned.

After an hour of this, the needles were removed. I felt so relaxed, I could barely walk. So I floated down into the ornate lobby. Then I hit the streets to get my ride, walking stronger than usual and making my own racket, becoming again a player in and not a listener to the urban symphony.

Gratitude showers our lives with grace

Gratitude showers our lives with grace.

Grateful and together, we celebrated on Thanksgiving. Now we move forward in grace to the next moment. And the next.

When I pause and breathe, "thank you" is a mantra to which I aspire. May the grace it brings continue to light a way through days dark or bright. Some that suck. Some that sing. A few described here.

Thank you for coming with me on this journey, written in this place of words and images. I am so grateful for you and wish for you lives wide awake to thankfulness and grace. Where every day is part thanksgiving

Christmas wolves

There is a story about a Cherokee grandfather teaching his grandson about life.

Grandfather says "two wolves inside me have fought all my days. One is the bad wolf, who is full of anger and pride and fear and envy. The other is the good wolf, full of peace and love and humility and kindness."

His Grandson asks "Which wolf will win?" Grandfather responds "Whichever one you feed."

Here's to feeding the good wolves at a time where they are desperately needed. Happy Holidays.

2017

Mindful through Terror

Sweat covered his whole body as he looked for the next handhold. Leaving the safety of the rope far behind, he was now clinging to the rockface like some sort of spiderman. Experience conquered his fear, but not by much. He focused and found the next hold, propelling himself over the top to safety in a sweaty exhausted heap.

These days, my experience of walking feels like climbing a rock face. The walker is like a rope. Without the rope, I search for handholds (chairs, tables, doors, etc.) and if I cannot find them, I walk while touching a wall. One day in national airport, I found myself without a wheelchair and needing the restroom. A fellow traveler offered me her strong forearm, a personal handhold. A saving grace.

My understanding of mindfulness practice includes something called the "sacred pause." This is a place where a short meditation can happen on the fly with a pause and the mind solely on the present. "I am standing up now." "I am taking hold of the walker." "I am leading with my left leg." "Step, pause, step, pause, step."

As I scale my daily mountain, mindfulness emerges from the effort. Walking becomes mediation which becomes quiet peace instead of dread. Don't look down. Just walk. If we pause, we may find this peace right now. And then the now can become richer as we crest our summits.

DELIGHT

Survival lives in sanity and sanity lies in paying attention.

The quality of life is in direct proportion to capacity for delight.

The gift of the delight is the gift of paying attention.

Julia Cameron

Featured in: **Julia Cameron Quotes via Quotefancy.com**

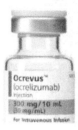

The "New" Drug for Progressive MS

The MS community is rightly excited about FDA approval of the first drug for progressive MS. The drug shows great promise for stopping new lesions and progression. It may even improve function for some.

However, it is a pity that it has taken so long for MS patients to have access to this kind of drug. The drug is almost identical to rituximab, which has been approved for many years for arthritis and other conditions. Because the patent was about to expire, the maker of rituximab did not do a phase iii study for MS, leaving rituximab without a formal indication for MS. As a result, many MS patients who could have benefitted from this drug were denied access because their insurance would only pay for drugs formally indicated for MS. Earlier studies had shown that rituximab had great promise for MS.

A year ago, my wonderful neurologist wrote an appeal to my insurer, who agreed to pay for rituximab for me. I have been taking it without incident, and I am hopeful that it will

stop further lesions, maybe even leading to some improved function. Given the formal indication for MS, I will likely switch to Ocrevus. This is wonderful, overdue news.

Keynote at Graduation for Doctors of Physical Therapy at Drexel U.

Thank you for that kind introduction. It is a great honor to be here with you today.

Before I get started, I want to thank Dean (Susan) Smith of the college of Nursing and health professions, Chairman (Glen) Williams of the department of physical therapy and rehabilitation services, and the faculty of the department. Thank you all for the opportunity to be here today. And a special thank you to Kevin Gard, Director of the DPT program and vice chair of the department and my friend, for the invitation to speak with you.

And to the GRADUATES, the class of 2017, I have the honor of being one of the first to say CONGRATULATIONS! Congratulations to you today, here with your families and friends. Congratulations on a job well done.

First, because I am a lawyer among doctors, I need to give you the gift of the best lawyer joke ever.

I understand the Drexel Laboratories are now using lawyers

rather than white mice in their research. This is for three reasons: lawyers are now more numerous than white mice, lab technicians feel closer to the white mice and there are just some things that white mice won't do.

I loved being a lawyer. I spent 14 years as a high-powered litigation attorney and had to retire in 2010.

I got help from a lot of people like you. I want to talk about my story and the hallmarks of courage in physical therapists that I have seen to be important.

My story begins on my first New York subway ride in 1985, with a new friend in my first week at Columbia College. I was new to the big city. The subway was so loud. It shook as if it would fall right off the tracks. It smelled like a men's restroom and was covered with graffiti.

This was New York in 1985. You weren't around yet but your parents knew Ronald Reagan as president. Ed Koch was mayor. And I was about to encounter the strongest man I've ever met.....in a moment that would today, in the time of ADA accommodations, blade runners, electric wheelchairs, and plentiful elevators — would not even happen.

The man near me on the subway sat in a rusty, banged up wheelchair. He wore an army shirt and pants that marked him as a Vietnam veteran. There were two things I noticed immediately about this guy. First, his legs were gone. Second, he had the biggest arms I have ever seen. Exposed by his sleeveless shirt, they were chiseled like a professional body builder's. He sat calmly as we rattled along, and when we reached our stop, he followed us closely, arriving at the bottom of a long flight of stairs.

Standing there in my jeans and new shoes bought for college, I felt a little ashamed to be near him. My puny arms and I hadn't gone to Vietnam. Hadn't done anything, really.

He turned to me and said "could you get my chair?" Before I even had a chance to say yes, he shifted his body and planted his hands on the filthy cement. As I looked on in amazement, he swung his torso up each stair, following with his arms and then up the next stair and the next and the next. I had to run with the wheelchair to keep up with him. When I reached the top, he climbed back into his chair, said thanks, and rolled away, leaving me open-mouthed, watching him move alone down the dark sidewalk.

This was a hero. A superhero, really. He did something on

those stairs that I had never seen or imagined. And he'd survived Vietnam, which for you today is a note in a history book, but for me was a blur of images from the nightly news I saw my parents watching in our living room long ago – gaunt prisoners coming home, napalm exploding over the jungle, the famous photo of the naked girl running toward the camera, terribly burned. For him, though: He had lost his legs there, he had made it back and he kept going.

I often thought of that veteran through the years – I had sort of a friendship with him in my mind. Even as I started law school far away from the grimy subway stairs, his image would roll around in my head over and over. Why did fate have him getting off at the same stop? Why did he choose me?

Then in 1994, in my third year of law school, my relationship with that veteran – that guy I thought of as a super hero – changed. It changed because at the age of 26, I was diagnosed with multiple sclerosis. And I got a whole new understanding of fate.

The summer before my diagnosis, numbness appeared in my upper legs after a long bike ride. I chalked it up to the seat and the ride. Then in the winter I fell hard on some ice in Boston's Back Bay. I noticed persistent numbness in my hands and arms, which sent me on a merry-go-round of doctor visits until a PT suggested I see a neurologist.

The most deadpan physician ever: "Your MRI shows several active lesions on your brain. What you have is clearly multiple sclerosis," he said, sitting in his small, university health care office.

MS was one of those scary diseases beginning with an "M" like muscular dystrophy or meningitis or multiple myeloma. But those were just a bunch of letters and Jerry Lewis and his kids. In shock, my mind felt like it was in a dryer on spin cycle. Images flooded over me of TV commercials featuring children in wheelchairs. Questions swirled. What did this mean for me? Would I be okay? Will it get worse?

Terrified, I glanced back and forth from the books on the doctor's shelf to his face. "The last law student I diagnosed with MS chose to lead a less stressful life. I think he is very happy and selling real estate on the North Shore."

Ever since I was a chubby kid working hard to get good grades, I had dreamed of going to Harvard Law. I remember eating too many Doritos and nerding out on "The

Paperchase" at the age of 13. By the age of 26, I had made it to the top 10% of my law school class. There was no way I was not going to be a lawyer and sure as hell I was not going to sell real estate.

Here let me tell him —

"Doctor, with all due respect, I am not going to go sell real estate."

Charging into law practice in Washington DC at one of the best firms in the country, and I did it while I had MS. The many MS relapses which all remitted. MS is an unpredictable, neurological auto immune disease. Your blood cells become confused and attack your brain and spinal cord and the lining around them. Scars called scleroses form, and your confused system can make you lose walking or arm function, go blind, endure pain and cognitive problems, and a whole list of other devastating symptoms. Most people start with the most benign form of the disease – relapsing remitting.

Intravenous steroids and new injectable drugs treated my recurring bouts of numbness. My hours were punishing. Sometimes I would go on a "war" schedule, arriving in the office at 4am and staying until eleven, day after day. [as noted in Kevin's introduction] I worked as a young lawyer on historic cases like the defense of President Clinton in the Senate Impeachment Trial.

My next big case led to a great story. Maybe even better over a drink at Westies.

As a young lawyer I got a case involving the Mafia. I couldn't believe I was going to get a chance to work on a case involving organized crime. But I did! This case was one where the people in the organized crime organization said that our client, who was a public figure, had been in cahoots with them and was dealing with them like they were associates or friends. Our job was to prove that they were not associates. We had to rebut the organized crime allegations that they knew my client.

So usually, when we have to rebut someone's testimony, at Williams and Connolly, we break them down piece by piece. But this witness that was coming at us was the saddest, most hapless mobster you have ever seen in your life. He walked in to give his testimony with no tie, no belt, and no shoelaces - so, a suicide risk.

I can't say much about the case. I will tell you it's a mob case and the witness' name was Nino Cucinotta. So Nino had just wanted to be a butcher. He'd come over from Sicily and worked in the local town.

By the way, to be clear, the case was not about Philadelphia, didn't happen in Phillie. If anyone here is concerned about this case I guarantee you it had nothing to do with Philadelphia.

In the town where he was, he was the driver for the local mafia boss. And he hated this guy. So finally, he's telling the story, on the direct examination by prosecutors, of how he finally went to jail, because somebody disrespected him in a bar. He walked out of the bar. He got his 357 magnum out of the car. He went back and put one in the guy's forehead and blew his head off and walked over and drove to his daughter's house and waited for the police to arrive, crying the whole time. And this is how this sad mobster ended up in jail. Wanting to shorten his jail time by testifying against our client.

At some point during his testimony, he got very, very emotional. He stood up on the stand and said, crying, "I just wanted to be a butcher and the local mob boss made me a whore." That's all they could get out of him for a total of five minutes. He had a total nervous breakdown.

So, I'm a young lawyer - I'm a second year lawyer - and I'm going like - Oh this is like TV, this is incredible. But the partner on our case, a very experienced defense lawyer, was asking me what to do about this guy. So, I said "well I don't think we should break him down, like we usually break people down. I think we should treat him with a lot of respect and maybe as if we are a little afraid of him 'cause he's so mental." So that's what we did. The other thing about this witness, Nino, was that he saw the Mafia everywhere. He said the local school principal was in the mafia, the milkman was in the mafia, the mayor was in the mafia - well actually the mayor was in the mafia. Everybody's in the mafia. So, the partner said to me "what should we say to this guy who sees mafia everywhere?" So, I thought for a minute and said: "let's ask him if it has ever been said of him that he sees the world through mob-colored glasses". The partner loved this and so we were going to use that the next day.

So, I'm very excited. I'm in a mob case. I've given good advice. They are going to use it the very next day.

The morning of the second day of the trial arrives. There in the lobby of this beautiful courthouse, all ready to go - advance team and paralegals are upstairs getting everything ready to go. I'm waiting for the partner and client to arrive in the lobby of the courthouse. People are milling all around the lobby. It's a big busy place. Well, then MS enters in. One thing MS does is it messes with your bowels. So, standing there in that lobby in my Brooks Brothers suit, already to go - everything I had eaten for the past three days came out of the back of me. All of a sudden, all at once. If you can imagine how bad this was, it is five times worse than you are imagining. It was devastating, just awful. Standing there in a crowded courthouse lobby, not knowing what to do, I think my career is over. I don't know what's going to happen. So, I started moving toward the door and then I spy the most unlucky cab driver in the history of cab drivers ever, sitting there waiting for a fare. I jump into his cab and throw $200 at him and beg him to drive me to my hotel, which - thank God - he did. I made it back to the hotel and I made it into the hotel before the partner and our client came out of the same door. I did not go down in history as the first associate to crap his pants at his first trial because nobody found out. I made it back to the case. They used my advice. We cross examined the witness. We won that part of the case and all was well.

So that's my story about the mafia. It's a story of resilience and a story of fate because it could have gone a different way. People could have shown up, people would have known. It also is a story of how MS has come to challenge me and I need to be ready at any time for the next challenge that's going to happen.

Years after the mafia trial, the veteran in his wheelchair reappeared, this time drawing closer to where I seemed to be heading. This time I did not think as much about him being a hero. This time all I could think about was his chair. At Johns Hopkins for a second opinion, the neurologist said that I would likely move along to secondary progressive MS. Where my relapses do not remit completely. Where I lose function over time. Driving home, I had to pull off the road as I collapsed into tears and terror, head against my steering wheel.

Another day, at a friend's fancy birthday bash, the bar thumped to the music on the dance floor. I was happily carrying two old fashions held high above the crowd. Suddenly I found myself flat on my face, not for the first time. Walking had become more difficult. My left foot dropped and caused falls. The left leg became a heavy, dead log after walking a mile or so. I started walking with a cane. I also started working hard with excellent physical therapists to hang on to as much as I could.

 In addition to difficulty walking, one of my other symptoms is heat sensitivity. On one of those D.C. days where 90° joins 100% humidity, I had the temerity to try and watch my kids' softball game. As soon as I stepped out of the car, my whole body started to numb, and my back began an electric ache. But, sick of being defeated, I doused myself with ice and staggered to the seats. The numbness deepened in my hands and legs. As I struggled, a black tunnel began to take over my peripheral vision. I thought of the veteran again. Once again, he was with me. The jungle had been hot. Stupid, cruel war. Stupid, cruel disease. Neither of us deserved what we had been handed. All we wanted was to move about our lives.

 As the years of hard work flew by, my disease became more progressive. I lost half of my walking distance each year. My left leg became a heavy dead log after only a little bit of walking. Without the help of my PTs, I am sure it would have gone away sooner.

One weekend I was in my big fancy office trying to write one paragraph of an email. I kept shuffling and reading the same handful of cases and articles. I could not write the paragraph. I wanted my brain to be quick and sharp. Now it felt dull and confused. I was terrified of how deep or long this new bad brain pattern might go. MS often results in significant cognitive slippage

 Soon after, in 2010, 16 years after my diagnosis, I hung it up. I went on full disability from law practice This was the hardest decision I ever made.

I sat in the examination room for my meeting with my neurologist, a noted Georgetown MS expert who had treated me for. "Doctor, how many years did you study to become what you are today?" he answered: Eight, if you include this residency." I said,

"I studied three years in law school and have worked hard for fourteen years to get where I am." I can imagine that you all have had this kind of conversation with a patient who is suffering a major loss. I needed him to hear me, because next I started to cry, and said: "You are about to witness the end of a brilliant legal career." My neurologist walked in with the completed disability form and found me sobbing with my head in my hands.

I just could not see a way that life would ever seem okay again. I could no longer do my life's work. I could barely walk. My financial future was completely in doubt. It felt like my sense of myself was under attack from all sides. I danced briefly with suicide. I tried to look to the veteran for inspiration, but all I could see was the chair.

As my disease progressed further, I continued to work with PT s and lived in fear that a big fall would leave me much more disabled. One night, just before Christmas, 2015, my left leg buckled underneath me and I fell hard, fracturing five ribs. The firemen carried me down my stairs on a special chair like some ancient king. I missed weeks of walks and workouts, and my walking slowed and shortened. I began using a wheelchair for any distance over about 20 yards.

I feel feeble and trapped, either wobbling on my feet with a walker or sitting in a chair. My legs just don't feel like they are mine any more. Most people don't face anything like this until their 70s or 80s. I wish for my strong legs. I even miss my old canes.

At times, the world seems to close in, and my self-pity gains strength. It's tempting to see just the chair. But the veteran's image won't allow much of it. His example allows no excuse, no despair, and no regret.

And so with the guidance of PTs, I work out every day to hang on to all I can. I am climbing my own set of stairs and I am not giving up. For me, taking any step is like his climbing a subway stair. I will walk carefully as long as I can, and when the walk is too long, I will use the chair.

I believe this is why I met the Vietnam that night so long ago. If he could fling himself up those awful stairs, my bumpy journey at least looks possible.

I have spent far more hours with physical therapists on my journey than with doctors. The PTs I have worked with are some of the most dedicated, caring people I have ever met. They have kept me walking through some hard times and helped ease the transition when I couldn't walk much anymore. They have helped me to feel like I did absolutely all I could do and to have no regrets over failing to do more.

I want to thank you for choosing to join this wonderful profession.

When you have MS, a lot of people talk to you about courage. I really love this quotation from poet David Whyte wrote this about courage:

"Courage is the measure of our heartfelt participation with life, with another, with a community, a work; a future. To be courageous is not necessarily to go anywhere or do anything except to make conscious those things we already feel deeply and then to live through the unending vulnerabilities of those consequences."

 And so let me ask you to consider:

What does courage look like when a physical therapist works with a patient like me?

Or with a child who lost a leg in a car accident? Or a 75 year old recovering from a stroke?

 It means listening, being present and open to the stories of our lives.

It means learning who we are and where we have been.

It means bringing all your excellent training and experience to bear on our situation.

It means facing the reality that you may not have the answer for us.

We may not improve. But that does not mean we can't be helped by you.

It means holding our sadness and frustration, even despair.

It means sitting in silence sometimes.

It means letting us use you — your strength your voice, your hands, your ears, your eyes.

It means setting small, creative goals for us to reach.

It means showing us when you are moved by our strength or our struggle.

Please have the courage to share your experience with us.

Thank you for listening to me share my experience here today.

And in the words of that courageous VETERAN, THANKS FOR GETTING MY CHAIR.

Get Busy Living

"Please call me asap" read the text from my neurologist. This could not be good news. I had recently enjoyed the two hours of thumping, clanging, and claustrophobia that is my yearly MRI. As an extra treat, the newbie tech stuck me twice before his more senior counterpart intervened with a perfect entry.

Unfortunately, I did not see my Doctor's 8:30pm text until the following morning, waking me up to fear and frantic texting to her. She is a friend and fellow MS board member, which is why she has my cell phone and texts me. She wrote that she was in the airport and would call me after she got through security. I stared at the phone for half an hour until she rang.

"Gil, I wanted to get to you before you saw the MRI report on the patient portal. It says you have three new active lesions, but I don't read it that way." If comfort could be colder than ice, that would have been mine at this moment. She went on to explain that some of the lesions look more like blood vessels to her. The conclusion was that there was only one new active lesion, a small one in a space where there have been lesions before.

Lesions are the enemy. They leave the scars or sclerosis that cause all the trouble. My image of it is that someone is burning a lit cigarette into my brain or spinal cord. If one is a brand-new location, that could bring new symptoms like pain or blindness.

We have limited measures to extinguish the cigarette. It will play out over time, but the effects can be catastrophic. I used to infuse with steroids, but eventually this caused osteoporosis. If I fall, I fracture.

So for the first time I am infusing intravenous immunoglobulin. This treatment is used for a number of diseases affecting the immune system. My understanding of it is a plasma-based immune booster. I will try anything once, even though it involves five days of three hour infusions. So far so good. In August, I will add the new drug Ocrevus which has shown promise.

My wife Lisa and I have our 50th birthdays this year. There will be much celebrating. I recently re-watched the movie "Shawshank Redemption" and recalled its famous line: We are getting busy living, not busy dying. Please join us.

Is this the end?

Although I use wheelchairs at work and for distance, my walker still supported those 50 or so paces from my door to a car or into a restaurant or around the house. Until two weeks ago.

At the beginning of a vacation in Bend, Oregon, my legs left me entirely. I needed assistance to move at all. While I could stand briefly, others had to physically manipulate my legs to walk. The wheelchair came indoors, and Lisa had to help me get into the restroom. Instead of enjoying her reunion in beautiful Bend with her best friends from college, we were distracted with my new symptom.

I have no idea why this happened. What I do know is that my mind fixed on the possibility that this was it: the moment I had to commit entirely to the chair. Lisa and I both grieved as we tried to put on brave faces for our friends.

With lots of hands helping, I managed without an electric wheelchair for the time being. But what about the next week? Lisa would return to work. I would have to negotiate stairs to even enter my house again.

I texted my neurologist, but she had no further
options. Even though I avoid steroids because of the
resulting osteoporosis, a three-day treatment had kept us an
extra day in Seattle when I had started losing my legs. We
had decided to fly instead of driving the 6 hours to Bend.
Having also recently completed an IV infusion, I had now
hit my system with every tool available for short term
recovery. The word came back from the doctor — she
would see me at our scheduled appointment in two
weeks. She had done all she could. I was on my own.

Mine is a progressive disease. Was this the new normal of
the progression? I had always wondered what the last step
before the full-time wheelchair looked like. I worried that
now I knew. My mind raced. How fast could we ramp the
house? Would we move to our first-floor bedroom? Did we
need to hire home health care? What will it be like to not
have the option of taking a few steps? Life was really
changing, maybe forever.

And then, suddenly, my legs came back. Just as quickly as
they had left. I stepped down off a stool where I had been
perched for about an hour, and my left foot could lift just a
bit again. My right leg kicked in strongly. I was walking

with the walker. The attack had lasted only a few days. My legs reverted to their usual, familiar difficulties.

We celebrated. My troubles turned out to be a temporary setback, not the death knell of walking at all. My fear turned to a longer timeline for the ramp and chair. Concern replaced terror. Sadness left for now.

Still, it was a terrifying few days. And a reminder of all the work we need to do in order to prepare for this situation to return. We will see this again, and next time we will be both more prepared for the loss of function and more hopeful about this loss being temporary. I have been warned.

The Master in the Kitchen

Every six weeks, my beautiful wife transforms our house for a religious experience. A special rug is placed in a sacred room, and a chair is placed on top of the rug. The rug is rolled out carefully and weighted down with talisman weights of a certain shape. The chair is positioned just so in the middle of the rug.

The house is cleaned even more than usual to a state of perfect preparedness. And then the day begins when the master arrives. She and her followers are the focus of the experience. Once she is set up, the day proceeds with her doing her magic upon person after person who come each six weeks to sit for a sacred hour in the special chair. Often others will arrive and wait their turn, talking about their lives and about what had happened in the last six weeks.

Sometimes friendships are formed and sometimes tears are shed. But the conversation with the person in the sacred chair is the focus of the room always, and the conversation about what is happening in the chair is the unspoken focus around which everything centers.

The chair is orange, a plastic chair from the upstairs study. But every six weeks it becomes the chair that holds the hope, fear, joy, and aspirations of every participant in this ritual. Master uses special tools to work her craft, and these tools are found in many places but do not work the same magic until wielded by the master. Her careful work transforms the people who sit. It renews their faith in their own worthiness and attractiveness. It allows them to dream and to change who they are during that one sacred hour.

If you have not yet guessed what art the master is working, I will tell you. I will tell you with the reverence that it deserves, a reverence that is often lost in our weary world. The master is a hairstylist.

Cul-de-sacs

I learned what the word "cul-de-sac" meant when my mother moved me and my brother to Bellevue, Washington, then a suburb of Seattle, now a major city in its own right. I had two different paper routes during two different periods of my adolescence in Bellevue. Both involved lots of turning around at the dead ends of suburban streets. Cul-de-sac is a much nicer word than dead end.

Life involves a lot of cul-de-sacs. Some cul-de-sacs feel familiar like my old paper routes. The bike and the yellow metal cart full of papers hitched up behind it just bump along. I know where the hardest hill will be and try to deliver as many papers as I can before I hit it because my ten speed does not shift low enough for that last hill. I feel silly walking the bike and cart up the slope.

Other cul-de-sacs feel unfamiliar but friendly, like the ones where a new friend might live in a house behind its basketball hoop on the side of the pavement circle at the end of the lane. The neighborhoods have names both quaint and anodyne – "Ardmore" reads the sign at the entrance to yet another ten blocks of similar homes.

Then others can be unfamiliar and unfriendly, more like really dead, dead ends. You're late. You're lost. You're turning this way and that, and you keep ending up in cul-de-sacs. It's raining. No one is home. The houses are dark.

Multiple sclerosis creates lots of these unfriendly kinds of cul-de-sacs for the people who live with it. My latest is a humdinger. Because of all the intravenous steroid treatments I had back when I had relapsing remitting MS, I have osteoporosis. Because I have osteoporosis, I need to take calcium supplements in the form of two Tums tablets per day. Because I take two Tums tablets per day and don't drink enough water (because I don't like going to the bathroom all day), I am now at risk for kidney stones. I hear that kidney stones are very, very bad things.

Another cul-de-sac: I'm also having an MRI on my kidneys at the end of this month to see whether they have been damaged by my bladder's over retention due to MS. If the findings are that my kidneys have been damaged or are being damaged, I will have to learn to self catheterize. That feels like a real dead end.

Doctors have urged self-catheterization on me for many years. For obvious reasons, I resist this idea. Not only do the mechanics of it seem beyond awful, the practice can give rise to infections. I've heard of out-of-the-box treatments like Botox, so maybe I will turn down Botox street and see what is there, always worried about ending up at the beginning again.

I am going to try to pedal my bike out of this mess by drinking lots of water. So if you have trouble getting me on the phone, you know where I'll be. The bathroom, trying like hell to escape these cul-de-sacs.

2018

All Will Be Well

All shall be well, and all shall be well, and all manner of thing shall be well...for there is a Force of love moving through the universe that holds us fast and will never let us go.

Julian of Norwich

Featured in Quotefancy.com

It Happened at the Seattle Women's March

We stood for women, my nine strong women friends and
me, waiting for the march to begin in Seattle. I was of course
sitting, not standing, in my wheelchair, with Lisa pushing
me along. We had been inside the park where the march was
to begin, but we moved out to the street with many of the
other marchers. It was hard to hear the people giving
speeches in the park, and we did not want to get trapped
when the whole crowd started to move. Everyone was

excited, clever signs all ready. My favorite read "I've seen smarter cabinets at Ikea!"

Then finally, after more than an hour of waiting, the security volunteers pushed us all to both sides of the street so the march could begin. Down came the sea of banners and tall painted figures towards us, led by about 50 Native Americans, some playing drums. First people, first in line.

Just to the side of the route, we were close enough to touch them. An older woman with a beautiful, careworn face and deep, piercing eyes singled me out. As she walked close by, she reached out and grasped my right hand gently. Saying nothing, she carried it with her for a few steps, looking into my eyes. Then, as the crowd moved along, we released each other's hands. Her eyes held an ocean of experiences in the life that she had led. Was she a shaman? A healer? Her message to me was crystal-clear: "I am with you." Because I will never forget that moment, she always will be. I am a very fortunate man indeed.

Gratitude

Grateful eyes look at each thing as if they had never seen it before and caress it as if they would never see it again.

Br. David Steindl-Rast

Featured in Quotefancy.com

Not MS?

My neurologist sounded frightened. "I usually get paged by my office for MRI results like this. I can't believe I missed them. I don't want you to see the slides." She said that these were the worst set of slides of my brain and spine that she had ever seen. I know what my brain and spine look like in MRI slides. My brain has lots of old white ghostly scars from prior attacks. My spine looks like a mouse took bites out of a it like a piece of cheese. I did not want to imagine what these slides could look like.

So we did what we usually do, starting a five-day steroid treatment. What was unusual was that I had no response to the steroids at all. I didn't get any better. This concerned my doctor, who was wondering whether the inflammation in my brain was due to something other than MS, like a rare brain infection or even lymphoma. We got another round of five days of steroids. Still no effect.

The next thing I knew, my neurologist was checking me into the hospital for tests and treatment. The test was a lumbar puncture, not the most pleasant experience. Every time the doctor missed his mark, electric shocks like enhanced interrogation coursed through my back. While we were waiting for the results, Lisa and I became more and more convinced that Lymphoma was a distinct possibility. Always a dangerous cold comfort, Google told us that there was a connection between lymphoma and MS

The day after the lumbar puncture, a phalanx of doctors appeared in my room, giving us the news that the tests showed no strange brain infection and that lymphoma would be incredibly unlikely. The good news was basically "you have really bad MS."

My neurologist put me on a treatment called plasmapheresis, the use of a centrifuge to separate my red blood cells from the plasma and replace the plasma with fresh plasma without the antibodies caused by MS. The treatment took about an hour and a half, and you can only have it once every other day. I needed to have five treatments, so the hospital stay added 10 days, finally resting at two solid weeks by the time I was done.

When people ask how I am doing, my big news is that I feel better, both physically and in terms of mood. I've had so many loving messages and visitors that my spirits have been buoyed above the highest wave.

One in particular, my dear friend Steve Toker, flew in from Dallas as soon as he heard that I was going into the hospital. An anesthesiologist, he's a former college Rugby teammate. He spent the four days pushing me to work out as much as I could. When I first was admitted, there was talk about me doing not only the plasmapheresis treatment but also some days of inpatient rehab at the end. Based on my level of activity, I think that the movement within my team toward asking me to do inpatient rehab started to abate.

So they let me take my new plasma and go. Home now, my latest MRI is no better. "Really bad MS" remains my acute condition. I have good days and bad days. The answer to the question "not MS ?" has met a resounding "NO" with extreme prejudice. A big YES to more MS.

Samurai

My fall on our wooden bathroom floor was surprisingly benign. Bruised a knee. The problem was that it landed me flat out on the floor at 3 AM in the morning when I didn't want to wake anyone up to help me. So, I was stuck. And my stuck-ness only increased when my bowels decided to unload on me at that moment. Still, I decided to wait it out, to stay on the floor until at least 6 AM so Lisa and the kids could get a full night's sleep. It may not have been the best plan.

Lying on the wood floor, I played a game with myself. I imagined that I was a samurai sleeping across the threshold of his Lord. Samurai slept on wood without anything else, I thought. So "Samurai! Bonsai!" Whatever. I was still stuck.

Finally, the clock struck 6 AM, and I couldn't take it anymore. So, I called out to Lisa, but she could not lift me off the floor. I had no legs and was completely stiff from lying there for so long. She lovingly cleaned me up and then called for her oldest son Sam to come and help me get up. It took both Sam and his younger brother Joey to get me off the floor. The bathroom smelled like you might imagine. They had to help me move my legs to get back to bed. I started to cry. Lisa started to cry, "This is so sad. It's just so sad," Lisa said.

Finally, they got me back into bed. Later, Lisa told me that as she was putting soiled clothing into the washer, Sam came up to her and said, "How are you doing mom?" Lisa started to cry once more. As this happened, Sam put his arms around her and said, "We can do this, mom. It's going to be OK." He held her tight for a long time. There was the real Samurai that day. A perfect combination of presence, strength, and grace.

Lessons from Mr. Rogers

"It's you I like,

It's not the things you wear,

It's not the way you do your hair–

But it's you I like

The way you are right now . . ."

This is the song that Mister Rogers sang to the five-year-old boy in the electric wheelchair.

Remember?

Lisa and I went to see the Mister Rogers movie. Using old footage and current interviews, the movie portrays a life well lived by a quiet and patient man, a man of music and of puppets, of curiosity and kindness.

One word that could be used to describe Mister Rogers and his neighborhood is "simple". They were as sweet and simple as the young children Mister Rogers was trying to reach. It takes an enormous amount of work to create such a simple space.

My life is becoming more and more simple these days. My writing has become more simple. The things that are important to me have become more simple. I don't hurry anymore.

Seeing the Mister Rogers movie made me feel better about this shift. To address these changes only with frustration would leave behind the important lessons that Mister Rogers worked so hard to teach us:

Listen.
Be kind.
Make believe.
Sing.
Go slow.

Value everyone regardless of their age or what they do.

Remain curious about the world and what is right in front of you.
Accept yourself and others just the way you are.

Remember that we all feel sad or angry sometimes.

Won't you be my neighbor?

The Swallow Battle

In the hospital for some impatient physical therapy, I suddenly spiked a high fever. The doctors told me and Lisa that it was pneumonia. They also said that they thought it was caused by me aspirating into my trachea when a swallow. An x-ray movie confirmed this. You could see the barium nectar that they gave me going right down my windpipe. It happened on every swallow.

I never knew that this kind of swallowing problem was a thing at all, much less something caused by MS. The doctor said that the muscle that controls the route of the food has been weakened by MS.

I was not ready to hear about the remedy that they prescribed:

All my food and drink from now on needed to be nectar thick, including water and any other drinks.

There are thickening agents that you can buy for drinks. Food needed to be puréed or of equivalent consistency. You have to cough each time you swallow in an attempt to clear the airway. Next step was a feeding tube they said.

I am 51 years old. I knew that MS could take almost everything away, but I never thought it would take away eating and drinking regular food and drinks.

I assumed that because my MS is progressive, this swallowing problem would never get better. To my surprise, three weeks later when they did another swallowing test with the x-ray video, no liquid went down my larynx. I have been faithfully doing the exercises the therapists prescribed: swallowing with your tongue in your teeth. Doing a hard swallow you bear down with all your might as you swallow. So I'm back in two normal life again. I can eat almost anything except salads and crunchy fruits with skins on them. I am very grateful to the excellent therapists at the University of Washington's Medical Center.

MS didn't win this battle

No pain No pain

At Thanksgiving I am grateful for several gifts that I have
been given. The first is that the pain sometimes caused by
MS has not hit me as yet. Your nerves get like electrical
wires, you could imagine the kind of pain this could cause.
Many people with MS suffered terribly from pain. Not this
fortunate man.   As you read in my last post, I am also very
glad to have my ability to eat return. Just in time for
Thanksgiving.

And above all, I am grateful form for my Wise, strong, and
Beautiful wife and wonderful Children and so many
supportive friends.

Happy Thanksgiving

2019

The old street

There is an old city street near my house. Ancient tree roots have cracked the pavement, leaving light and air for grass to grow out of the openings. Potholes are everywhere, some as large as manhole covers, others so deep they show the old brick under the pavement. To all of this, speed bumps have been added, as if they were really needed, which they are not.

For me, 2018 was like navigating this street in a wheelchair. I am currently sitting stuck in the largest pothole. Having tried every one of the fourteen available disease modifying therapies, I'm left with none that have worked and a brain inflamed for more than a year now. I am currently moving through a six month round of chemotherapy, a Hail Mary pass by my frustrated neurologist.

The MRIs all show more and more new lesions. Each has brought its own charming new symptom.

When 2018 started I could walk at least 50 or so paces. One sunny day, my trainer and I made it all the way uphill to our local park. Now, I have not left the wheelchair for weeks. I can't even stand up on my own.

My vision has deteriorated to a point where I can't even think about reading normal sized print. I have to rely on enlarging all text on my iPad.

My voice has become week and scratchy, as if I had laryngitis. I have a home health aide who gets me ready for the day and another who gets me into to bed.

I have made peace with these changes, and I realize the old city streets may never be paved smooth again. I work on the things that can be helped, and I try to accept the things that

cannot. When I get the decision wrong in terms of what I can work on, my mortal enemy regret circles around. I can live in regret over not having worked out more or not having done more. Most days I can easily dispatch these feelings of regret by reminding myself of all the things that I did do and how much they helped for as long as they could. What I do know is that every day you will find me trying to make my way around and over the speed bumps and potholes.

Purpose

As my acute troubles continue – chronic brain inflammation with new lesions, losing my vision, inability to feed myself, and confusion- I have been thinking about purpose.

I read *Man's Search for Meaning* which is a famous book written by a psychologist, Viktor Frankl, who survived the holocaust. He observed that the people in the concentration camp who had a purpose survived while others did not. His purpose was to reconstruct a manuscript which he had written but that had been taken from him when he arrived at the camp.

I believe the best purpose for my life right now is to work on mindfulness and expanding my ability to accept and live with change.

I have been listening to lectures on mindfulness and one of the lectures I enjoyed was about gratitude.

Recently, the weather was absolutely perfect. I sat for a couple of hours by myself in my wheelchair on my back deck and enjoyed the light breeze. I thought about how fortunate I am. The things that I thought about were the fact that I can breathe and I am living here with my wife who is alive and sharing a life with me. I thought about the many friends and family who are in my life. I have support every day.

Recently, my cousin and his wife flew out from Alexandria, Virginia for a couple of days just to say hello. I have a friend flying in from Texas next week and in August, my annual reunion of rugby teammates will be brought to me in Seattle for the first time instead of at my friend's cabin in Canada.

My family, including the older generation who are all quite healthy, are a source of enormous support. I also have many, many friends and supporters at Williams and Connelly in Washington DC where I have worked for more than 20 years.

One of my law partners flew out for the weekend just three weeks ago. We watched the basketball finals together. I began thinking of all the families who on Memorial Day are mourning the loss of a loved one. I am grateful to those who have chosen to defend our country.

Although the journey towards mindfulness is something

that I've been working on for quite some time, I am going to redouble my efforts. Wish me luck.

Let's Dance

It has finally happened. After years of treatments and MRIs.
After two separate sessions, each lasting ten painful days, of
the blood washing treatment called plasmapheresis. After
the last-ditch effort of six months of chemotherapy, I am left
with the last MRI showing what the results of all this are.
Will the chronic inflammation and lesions that have plagued
me and brought a dramatic worsening of my condition for
almost two years start to calm down?

The neurologist said that chemotherapy should always affect
an MS process by improving this kind of lesion presentation.
We got the results this week and after all this treatment, they
are a little better, but ultimately inconclusive. There appears
to be some lessening of inflammation, but many active
lesions still appear.

My very perplexed and concerned neurologist has consulted
with neurosurgeons and neuro-oncologists in a charmingly-
named group called The Tumor Panel. I am the most
complicated case in the University of Washington MS Clinic,
and my neurologist has put my case out on the wires to
neurologists all over the world for consultation.

The neuro-oncologist is recommending a biopsy of my brain–the tissue down deep inside–to see whether this presentation is a rare form of brain cancer instead of multiple sclerosis behaving strangely and badly.

We met with the neurologist to discuss the options. One is to go back to the powerful drug Tysabri, which I took for eight years back in Washington DC. During that time, I had no new lesions, but it's unclear how taking the drug for that long a period could affect someone. This drug has the possible side effect of causing a dangerous infection called PML–progressive multifocal leukoencephalopathy.

It eats your brain. This infection is deadly in one in five people who contract it. It does irreversible damage. Data on people like me who had been on the drug for a long time and then returned to it shows that these steps result in a one in 100 chance of contracting PML.

As I said to the disease in my speech at the wonderful MS Society award dinner several years ago, "You wicked disease. Do you not realize that we have thousands of angels arrayed against you? Do you not understand the fact that if you strike one of us down, 10,000 will rise to take their place?" All those supporters who gathered that night: my law partners who flew out from Washington DC, my beautiful extended family and many friends, including those from the MS Society and others who are in contact with me almost every day, they were all there to be present for this moment. I am so fortunate to have such support and I'm so ready to take this next step.

It will take six months to see whether this drug which worked so well a long while ago will help to reduce the inflammation and show that the lesions are due to MS, thus avoiding for now the need to undergo a deep brain biopsy. I will start this monthly infusion soon, with constant monitoring for signs of PML.

It is time for courage. I have decided that since multiple sclerosis has decided to mess with me so much, I am going to rename it from MS to MF. This change is inspired by the powerful movie *Gleason* in which a star college football player played for the New Orleans Saints and famously blocked a punt that help the Saints win the Super Bowl. He made a documentary about his descent into ALS so that his son could come to know him after his likely death.

Like mine, his wife was an incredibly strong presence, and at one point in the movie, says about the disease "This is a motherfucker." So MF, let's dance.

Our Summer on the Bay Downtown

Elliott Bay is the part of Puget Sound that forms the harbor of the city of Seattle. It is lined with piers, restaurants and tourist attractions such as the Seattle Aquarium and The Great Wheel. Toward the northern most end of the harbor stand grain elevators and docks where the huge cruise ships bound for Alaska take on their passengers. Just south of all this activity sits the iconic Edgewater hotel, a Seattle institution where once the Beatles stayed, leading to a locally famous picture of their four heads poking out the window over the water. The motto of the Edgewater is: "Fish from your window." The hotel boasts a roomie bar and lovely dining room, both looking out large windows immediately onto the water.

My wife and two of her girlfriends have made a tradition of celebrating their birthdays over lunch at the bar. One day in the late spring they decided to bring along their husbands for one of their lunches.

 A very good time was had by all, and at the end, looking around the scene on this bright beautiful day, my amazing wife Lisa shared an idea: "I think Gil and I should come here every Friday in the summer and spend the night. We can have drinks in the bar in the middle of the day with one set of friends and then later have dinner with another group. "

And so it began. Lisa negotiated a favorable rate on one of the beautiful rooms. We rented a Hoyer lift and asked the hotel to store it for our use. My caregiver Maria came in the evening after dinner. She used the Hoyer to lift me out of the wheelchair and onto the bed. We found in the morning that she and Lisa together could slide me from the bed into the wheelchair without the Hoyer.

On our visits to the bar in the afternoon, my too-frequently repeated joke was that the catheter that has been inserted into my bladder had resulted in a need for flushing by drinking the recommended 3 liters of liquid per day. My joke was that the particular liquid was not specified and that, "Hey, tonic and gin are liquids."

The Fridays arrived and punctuated the Summer with laughter. The staff in the hotel and the restaurant and bar became our new friends. Small traditions arose. The bar offered a Cuban sandwich at lunchtime, and of course wonderful Seattle fish options for dinner.

Boats came by on the sparkling Bay as we sat in the bar, which itself seemed like our great big boat. Every so often, one of the boats from the company formerly called Seattle Harbor Tours appeared, usually prompting a story from me about the Summer after my Columbia University freshman year that I spent cleaning those boats at 5 AM every morning down on the dock.

This was the summer when I bought a used BMW motorcycle and rode it from Seattle back to New York City for my sophomore year at Columbia. Because Robert Persig, who wrote the book, *Zen and The Art of Motorcycle*

Maintenance, had been a professor at Montana State University, I made the pilgrimage to Bozeman and went to the MSU bookstore to buy a copy.

While looking at the shelf for the book, a copy of *Siddhartha* by Herman Hess fell into my hand and changed my life. Siddhartha was the son of a rich lord (brahmin). Handsome and brilliant, he was not satisfied by the wise elders and their teachings, or even by the teachings of the Buddha himself, who Siddhartha met. He resolved to experience life, becoming a rich merchant, a gambler, a lover and father.

I decided that, like the seeker Siddhartha, I would pursue everything that life had to offer. I dove headlong into Rugby and College, engaged in protests and got arrested twice by the NYPD. I played around in Manhattan after graduating Columbia and lived with 3 Rugby buddies in Hell's Kitchen (now Clinton). In law school I was taught by Lawrence Tribe, one of the foremost scholars of constitutional law and the lawyer who argued Bush v. Gore twice before the Supreme Court. My second-year moot court argument was judged by none other than the late Archibald Cox, the Watergate special prosecutor who's firing by Richard Nixon, triggered what became known as The Saturday Night

Massacre—a cascade of DOJ resignations that was one of the stones in the avalanche leading to Nixon's resignation. Cox told me that I had argued well.

After graduation, I clerked for judges in Honolulu and Seattle. And then had the unbelievable good fortune of working with some of the most legendary lawyers in the country at the law firm of Williams and Connolly in Washington DC. I worked on the defense of William Jefferson Clinton—the second impeachment trial in American history—drafting some lines that when spoken on the Senate floor by partner Nicole Seligman were the only lines shown by the news networks for that day of the trial:

"Now is the moment when the failure of the managers proof, the wise prescriptions of the framers, and the best interests of the nation all come together to move this great body to dismiss these articles of impeachment. You have listened. You have heard. The case cannot be made. It is time to end it."

Back at home in Old Town Alexandria, I walked down to the Potomac and around lovely rowhouses with my three beautiful children: two sharp, funny, curly red-haired girls and a smart, sturdy boy. The twins in their double jogger stroller stopped foot traffic on the sidewalks of King Street. Our Scottie dog, Clyde, did his share too. At the crest of this wave I had a full life and a career that I loved. Multiple Sclerosis took it all away. A blaze of fortune's white light, landed me with the love of my life in a wonderful home in Seattle.

In the last chapter of his life, Siddhartha found peace

working a ferry across a wide river. I plan to listen and learn from where I am.

What I have learned so far is that everything is connected — the motorcycle, the glistening water, my glorious wife and our friends — and that you get closer to peace the more you can love what is- breathing in, breathing out, listening to the rain on my back porch and sitting in this damn wheelchair.

Reasons for Optimism

Jaded by the failure of so many MS drugs, I have struggled to be optimistic about any. A few years ago, I was encouraged by Ocrevus, the first drug ever developed for progressive MS. KING 5 News even interviewed me about it. It didn't work for me.

The one MS drug that ever worked was Tysabri. I took it back in DC for eight years.

My then-doctor took me off Tysabri. She was worried about what it might do after eight years, fearful that it could cause the deadly infection PML (Progressive Multifocal Leukoencephalopathy). I had no progression or lesions during that entire time. She was hopeful that new drugs like the brand-new oral drug Tecfidera would pick up where Tysabri left off. None did.

After she ended Tysabri, wave after wave of new symptoms trampled me. I went from walking with a cane to struggling with a walker and then fulltime in a wheelchair, with terrible burning pain below my knees in the evenings.

Now having completed my first two monthly doses of Tysabri, supporters are remarking on my clarity of speech and writing. Many of your kind comments on the last blog post said that it was the best-ever. I recently reclined my wheelchair and pushed myself up six inches with no assistance.

In four months, an MRI will show whether Tysabri has affected the inflammation attacking my brain for more than two years.

It takes no imagination or effort to observe this positive reality. Worries about the upcoming MRI results retreat.

In my work on mindfulness, I open to what arises: sounds, sensations — including pain — and then, of course, thoughts. They arrive like waves on the ocean. Occasional waves of reality-based optimism are appearing.

One Day in the Senate Impeachment Trial, 1998

I worked on the team defending President Bill Clinton in the 1998 impeachment trial in the Senate. As one of the junior lawyers I helped get the speech by Williams & Connolly partner Nicole Seligman ready for the Senate floor. She was to make a speech in support of the Defense motion to dismiss the articles of impeachment at the close of the evidence presented by the house managers. Nicole Seligman is a brilliant lawyer, and her draft speech set forth a well-reasoned argument citing the relevant authority. However, it was very dry.

As I read it, I felt that it needed a hook. I took out my pen and wrote carefully in the margin above one paragraph: now is the moment when the failure of the managers' proof, the wise prescriptions of the framers and the best interests of the nation all come together to move this great body to dismiss these articles of impeachment. You have listened. You have heard. The case cannot be made. It is time to end it.
The lines I wrote made up the only part of that day played by all the major news networks that night.
Later in the trial I sat with the staffer from the White House who was playing the video clips from the deposition of

Monica Lewinsky. We were sitting at a little table tucked on the side of the Senate floor. David Kendall was standing in the well of the Senate in front of Chief Justice William Rehnquist making an argument. As Kendall spoke, Republican senators shouted curses: "F/// you Kendall!"

2020

We Here Know Why Honor Matters

At the Red Sox game shortly after the Boston Marathon bombing, slugger David Ortiz spoke:

"All right, Boston," Big Papi said, clapping his hands. "This jersey that we wear today, it doesn't say 'Red Sox.' It says

'Boston.' We want to thank you, Mayor [Thomas] Menino, Governor [Deval] Patrick, the whole police department for the great job that they did this past week."

"This is our fucking city. And nobody's going to dictate our freedom. Stay strong."

Regardless of politics, Americans agree about honor. The recent book, "Why Honor Matters", by Tamler Sommers, shows this; as does a certain law firm I know in Washington DC.

We spoke to the Mafia lawyer as the sun set blood red out his office window over Hoboken

Tommy Patrizzo was an indicted murderer from Northern New Jersey whose legitimate company built the little subway in the Newark Airport. Larosa called Patrizzo from his office. Larosa had represented Paul Castellano, who was the overall Boss of the New York crime families and was gunned down by John Gotti's men at Sparks Steakhouse in 1985. I looked out the office and saw the distinctive, very bald head of Bruce Cutler, the lawyer who kept John Gotti from being convicted on multiple murder charges in multiple trials earning Gotti the Knick name "the Teflon Don". That was a little scary to see Bruce Cutler's bald head.

We were explaining to Tony Larosa that we needed the transcripts for use in our defense of Arthur Coia, the President of the Laborers' Union. We were defending Coia against charges brought in an internal disciplinary proceeding in a process that Coia, the reformer of the Union, had initiated at the suggestion of Williams and Connolly, to expel all those who, in the language of the code that had been adopted for the process, had associated with known mob figures. Coia's own process had come after him and was trying to remove him from the Union because he had allegedly associated with organized crime figures. Patrizzo responded that he would release the transcripts to us if we could do something for him. The familiar Quid Pro Quo which itself would clearly have violated the Union code; and to which we responded "No". The judge in our Union process was the respected former US Attorney of Philadelphia, named Peter Vira. At the end of our meeting as the sun set over Hoboken in the distance, Larosa leaned over the desk (and I always believed that Larosa who was not a tall man was somewhat elevated when he sat behind that desk, didn't know why, but perhaps a small ramp behind the desk) so Larosa leaned to me and Howard (retired Ambassador to Belgium – Howard Gutmann) and said; "Your guy from Philadelphia is going to F —- you." At that point I wanted to say: "Howard, could we go now?" The transcripts we were looking for were the cross examination of the witness who the Union prosecutors-retired Assistant United States Attorneys -were using against Arthur Coia.

The name of the witness was Sal Michiotta. His nickname

was "Fat Sal". Fat Sal had successfully testified in trial after trial of Mafia murder cases. He had been put on the stand by a Federal prosecutor – Andrew Weissman- who would later be one of the lawyers in the team that Bob Mueller put together and is now a commentator for MSNBC.

The Union prosecutors dropped the charge relating to the New York Mafia when they learned that one of the participants at the alleged meeting with Coia was dead at the time.

What can we do?

This is the question that we ask ourselves in this historical moment. This is also the question that Brendan once asked me and it saved my life.

The following is the transcript of a video made for the MS Society, May 25, 2020.

"Hi, my name is **Gil Greenman**, and it's a great honor and pleasure to be speaking with you all today. I graduated in the top 10% of my class from The Harvard Law School. To great good fortune I got a job at Williams and Connelly in Washington, D.C. I served as a young lawyer on the defense of President Clinton in the impeachment trial. I loved my career, I really did. I was diagnosed with relapsing remitting Multiple Sclerosis. A few years after I made partner I was walking with a cane.

I was working on my last case and I was trying to write an email on a complicated matter and I just could not write the email. I took a very deep breath and went to Sullivan's office and told him "Something's wrong". He said something, I'll never forget it. "This could have happened to anyone. It's happened to you. What can we do?"

Allison Krehbiel, Director for MS Navigator services, National MS Society:

"People living with MS have skills and talents that just should not be wasted. Employees know when their employer is being supportive both to themselves but to their colleagues as well, and the benefits of that are huge. Living with MS can be a challenge and reaching out for support is an important thing to do. You definitely are not alone in this journey in figuring out how to remain engaged at the workforce. "

Gil: When they said "What can we do?" I had no fear to share with them what was going on. I asked for a part time job working on electronic discovery and working on educational programs for the young lawyer. So they created a title for me: Senior Consultant for Discovery and Professional Training. A title that I still enjoy to this day.

It was enormous. Many organizations are trying to become humane. That is the word that I think is most apt for this.

Different things happen to different people and we have to address them with humanity.

On Deck

Yesterday I was getting ready for a hot day on my back deck while Dr Lisa practices her psychology in the front of the house inside. Good day went well and was warm but livable. Oscar and Oliver kept me company.

I Stood up!

On July 1st, I stood up for the first time in 2 years and 7 months. This was a miracle here for me. As a believer, I do believe that it was brought about by prayer; the prayers of all of you

It also happened because of the shifting, unpredictable force of the disease, continued work by me, Lisa, and my team to keep some strength, and the effects of the revolutionary drug Tysabri.

It underscores what we must remember always: do all you can to be ready when the moment arrives and then bring your best. Trust in love, faith, and good fortune. Always.

What We See

We see them when we close our eyes.

Points of light and shapes and texture like well cared for fur or feathers. When there is light beyond us, they look different than when it is dark. I have struggled to find the right word for them because dot is too dark and my son's good word "refractions" is accurate but too long. I finally settled on "friends". My good fortune allows this name.

Because of the optic neuritis, they are always now in my field of vision with eyes open. They move and dance and create an effect much like looking through a filter that turns everything into an impressionist painting. It is sometimes distracting, sometimes quite lovely. I can read through it, and I can see your faces but not with perfect clarity. Think Monet's hay stacks.

What I realized was that the friends are like all of us, shining and dancing around. For me, now they are everywhere. With cells forming bodies and atoms forming everything, of course they really are. We know this but do not live in it. Maybe when we pass away, it will be this, continuing on together and separate, like the stars throughout the universe.

211

This knowledge, this vision, lives with me every moment now. Every interaction, whether with a fellow human or our dogs is experienced through this lens of dancing light.

Rules of the 100 Year Flood

As we move along through this amazing and terrible time, a few lessons have emerged to me as being particularly important. On my kitchen wall we have a framed copy of "Jefferson's rules" — common sense and attractive -- notwithstanding the facts that their author was a slave holder who engaged in some bad conduct.

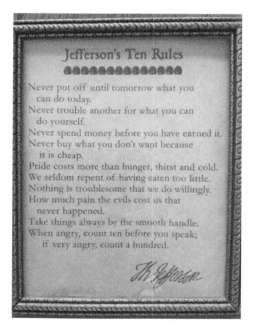

Here's an offering of some of these and then some of my own:

Jefferson's rules include:

If you are angry, count to 10 before you speak, and if very angry, count to 100.

Don't buy what you don't want because it is cheap.

One seldom suffers from having eaten too little.

Take things always by the smooth handle.

Here are my offerings:

If it ain't broke, don't fix it.

Go big or go home.

So-So is truly OK for now.
Don't poke the bear.

Keep calm and carry on.

Keep your powder dry.

Better to keep silent and be thought a fool than to open your mouth and remove all doubt. Thank you, President Lincoln.

If possible, take a year before you make any life-changing decisions after a death or divorce. By then, life will have revealed itself more clearly.

"When people tell you who they are (trust but verify), and when they show you who they are, believe them." Maya Angelou said this.

Train, train, train, and practice, practice, practice, at what you do just like David slinging stones to ward off wolves from his flock of sheep. Then, when the moment arrives, bring all of the training and practice to what you're doing. If you do, you just might kill Goliath with one shot.

Be kind. Be kind. Be Kind. This is attributed to Henry James as a statement he made to his three sons before they left to seek their fortunes.

Listen lovingly and carefully to all who you value.

Breathe in and breathe out, grateful for your ability to do this.

Combat Meditation

I am not a meditation teacher, nor do I make any claim to be an authority on the subject. For more than 20 years I have practiced some, have listened to some guided meditations and have attended talks on the subject. For me, it always comes back to this basic technique, for use when a lot is happening, inside or outside of you:

1. Practice covering the entire breath with your attention, from before the beginning of the in-breath through after the end of the out-breath.

2. Count one slowly on the in-breath and two slowly on the out-breath

3. Continue counting. Take a deep breath on nine

4. Repeat counting to 10 two times as slowly as you can.

If you lose count, simply begin again at one

Ton of Bricks

One day I was coming out of my bedroom on my way to my spot in the kitchen where I spend all day long watching TV, making phone calls and bouncing emails. All of a sudden, it hit me like a ton of bricks: I will never walk again. I might stand up, but I will never walk again. Sudden, crushing realization of this truth, which I know and have pushed off. That's it.

Vulnerability

is not a weakness, a passing indisposition, or something we can arrange to do without, vulnerability is not a choice, vulnerability is the underlying, ever present and abiding undercurrent of our natural state. To run from vulnerability is to run from the essence of our nature, the attempt to be invulnerable is the vain attempt to become something we are not and most especially, to close off our understanding of the grief of others. More seriously, in refusing our vulnerability we refuse the help needed at every turn of our existence and immobilize the essential, tidal and conversational foundations of our identity.

To have a temporary, isolated sense of power over all events and circumstances, is a lovely illusionary privilege and perhaps the prime and most beautifully constructed conceit of being human and especially of being youthfully human, but it is a privilege that must be surrendered with that same youth, with ill health, with accident, with the loss of loved ones who do not share our untouchable powers; powers eventually and most emphatically given up, as we approach our last breath.

The only choice we have as we mature is how we inhabit our vulnerability, how we become larger and more courageous and more compassionate through our intimacy with disappearance, our choice is to inhabit vulnerability as generous citizens of loss, robustly and fully, or conversely, as misers and complainers, reluctant and fearful, always at the gates of existence, but never bravely completely attempting to enter, never wanting to risk ourselves, never walking fully through the door.

David Whyte

Featured via **Quotefancy.com**

Never Surrender

Life is a struggle. This we know. I would like to invite anyone who is reading this to send me your story of struggle and maybe overcoming.

My email is Gilgreenman@gmail.com

I look forward to hearing from you.

First Story of Overcoming

My dear friend Ken Lopez offered me the story below. I am grateful to him and for him:

Written august 31st, 2020

After a stroke on march 5, 2020 (plus subsequent meningitis, sepsis twice, pneumonia, and blood clots in both legs), today, after six months of hospitals/rehab facilities, I leave — for good. I am grateful to be alive. I am grateful to be in much better shape. I am grateful for my (continued) recovery.

I have met so many heroes along the way. Thank you to each and every person who was there for me. Some of you played a direct role saving me; some of you played a role in my

220

recovery, and some of you just took the necessary precautions, so I never got covid on top of all of this. From the bottom of my heart, thank you, no matter what your role was.

I want to extra-thank some specific people (by initials only – if you want to tag yourself, you may). My heartfelt gratitude goes out to: ljs, vat, mo, dps, rr, rdl, jh, sh, mi, lt, jg, cw, gg, tl, knw, jb, ag, gvs, sm, gj, tr, ml, alt, lr, rg, mj, dc, hk, nk and finally dmcn, especially you, without whom, none of this would be possible.

I did not get to decide how I would live my first life, in advance, but for this second life, I do. With this unique opportunity comes unique responsibilities, in my view.

To my friends, to the people I love, to my family, and to anyone else I touch along the way, I make these seven promises for my second life.

I promise to move forward with gratitude — always, every day. I don't remember much from the first couple of months, but I remember the night of my stroke. There I was, lying on the floor at home alone, unable to move, unable to speak, unable to summon help, and unsure if help would ever come. Just a few hours later, it did. I will use that uniquely juxtaposed moment of ultimate fear and ultimate relief to summon gratitude, whenever and wherever a need it, forever.

I promise to let patience and forgiveness be my guides. If I can pull this one off (it is the most ambitious of these promises), I will no longer be vulnerable to stress, and, after all, it was the stress that nearly killed me. Don't be blown about by every wind, as they say.

I promise to never again lash out at those I love — just because I feel somehow slighted. "Pause, respond, and don't react," is my new motto.

I promise to respect life and my body, especially while working on my recovery and physical therapy from my new home. That said, I plan to work harder than ever, especially on my new company, OurHistoryMuseum (details soon).

I promise to keep loving as if a have never been hurt before. I take big risks, so I get hurt often. But each time I love again, I do so fearlessly. I love this about me. I will continue to be that person.

If one's friends are like change in your pocket, where higher denominations equal deeper relationships, I promise to spend more time with my quarters than my pennies. That requires effort — from both of us. Let's live like I almost died — because I almost did.

So many people have been so kind to me — nurses, doctors, therapists, support staff, roommates, friends, employees, family, and even strangers — particularly early on when I behaved like a jerk. I'm deeply sorry for all of that. From now on, when in doubt, I promise to reflect all the kindness that has been shown to me and, instead, to simply try to do the next 'kind' thing.

At any point, I invite each of you to pull me aside and hold me accountable for any of these promises. They are each aspirational, so at all times, you can expect progress, not perfection.

This stroke has humbled me, and I have lost everything. But in reality, and I can only now see this, I did not lose anything compared to what I have gained. Thank you, world, for my second chance, my stroke of luck as it were. I promise to make the most of it.

Ken Lopez, ken@ourhistorymuseum.org

2021

Sweet Dog Story

I began spasming uncontrollably one morning. The only way to make this stop before it just runs its course is to give me a hug. My caregiver who was also in the kitchen came over and gave me a hug. Suddenly, we looked down and noticed that each dog was up on a separate foot as if to say "I am helping" or "what's wrong, dad?"

So sweet. my dogs are my protectors and they gave a moment of pure love.

Ballard Landmark, Long Term Care, on Friday

First came the cane which I walked with for years and years. Next came the push chair which did not last long. And finally the 500 pound electric wheelchair, where I sit today and every day.

My whole life felt like an effort to forestall this moment.

I sit in this wheelchair in my beautiful house in the kitchen where I can see the big TV that we have put up on the wall. I sit here all day, every day, and do not move around very much. We put in a lift so that when I want to go down to the street level I can, with the help of another.

This way of living no longer offers enough stimulation or care.

It is time to move into a long-term care facility.

The community we found is special. It seems to be home to many interesting people and is located in one of the hippest neighborhoods in Seattle. I move in this week on Friday

Filled with lots of competing emotions, Lisa and I trust that this is what love looks like today.

A Unicorn

After almost 3 weeks at the Ballard Landmark, I would say that Lisa and I found a unicorn, a lovely beast of precious price. There is a gym where I can work out in the morning before going to have some scrumptious breakfast in the dining room. There is access to a hip neighborhood in Seattle that has many tremendous restaurant options. There are lots of programs for the benefit of the residents, like a New York Times headline discussion and trivia and a spiritual group. I had two nice hour-long conversations with Irma who is 97

years old and does the biographies for the incoming new

residents. It is like a high-end cruise ship. So in answer to

any question what do you think of long-term care? I would

say that I like it very, very much. My only complaint is that

I don't see Lisa as often. But that was always part of the deal

in moving to long-term care and we will handle it. Some

happy days, some sad days.

Shotgun Shack

When I was 10 years old, my parents moved us to a low-income housing project called Southmoor. It consisted of about 200 white row houses up a long hill from the street at the bottom. I could walk to my new elementary school which was called Richmond elementary and there I had a new teacher named Jim Hamilton. So much to say about Hamilton. A MASH medic during the Vietnam war, he was a big bear of a guy with powerful arms. He clearly enjoyed teaching kids who were 9-10. He had a big paddle near his desk and it was all decorated with tape of various kinds. When students had their birthday while they were in school, Hamilton would paddle them as many years as they were old. I was very happy to have a July birthday. When the Iran hostage crisis was dragging on and on, I heard Jim Hamilton say "if we had Barry Goldwater as president this would never have happened." Richmond elementary served the Southmoor projects as well as some foothill areas.

These people were referred to as hill people. This one foothill kid's name was Jimmy Walker and Jimmy refused to bathe. I never noticed anything wrong with Jimmy but Hamilton had a bee in his bonnet. One day he said "OK, Walker, I warned you about this," and Hamilton grabbed him by an arm, took him screaming down to the janitors closet, and washed Jimmy with cold water in a janitors bucket.

One of the things that Jim Hamilton and some other teachers did with us fifth graders was to take us on a weekend to a small house in a town in West Virginia called Sissonville. We went and stayed in this house and played games in the yard and took hikes. One day, one kid and I took a hike together and we moved from hollow to hollow finally realizing that we were lost. About that time, we stumbled on a shack that had cans around it with buckshot shot through them.

I was terrified. Finally, after seemingly hiking in circles, we rounded the top of a hollow and saw houses. Fortunately, there was a kind man who knew where we were staying and drove us back. Years later, I heard that this kid with whom I took the hike had almost died because someone had put poison ivy in his marijuana. I had a risky childhood in West Virginia but I survived through good fortune always.

Miracle Worker

My leg pain has been worsening dramatically lately. It is like electric burning below my waist if I get touched. There has to be a lot of touching by my caregiver, Maria, when the Hoyer lift is being used to get me in or out of bed.

Just the other day, Maria came up with a different way of raising my legs to get the Hoyer straps underneath. She grabbed my feet with the shoes on and did not even touch my legs at all. This reduced my pain by about 80%. A minor miracle which had Maria as its agent. She is a powerful angel. And I am a fortunate man.

Luxury

If you ever want to know the definition of the word "luxury," try having a warm towel on your face every morning. It is just hot enough to be on the edge of too hot but it's never really too hot. I have it put on my face as I wake up in the morning. So dreamy.

Please Contribute

Fifteen years ago, the medication Tysabri was developed using research dollars supplied by the MS society. Tysabri kept me free of new lesions and minimized my progression for more than a decade. I was taken off of Tysabri by a neurologist concerned about the powerful side effects of the medication and the development of the deadly PML virus. Off the medication, I experienced tremendous progression. Because of this progression, I am now full-time in a wheelchair. Since starting Tysabri again, my progression has stabilized and I feel better. This is the powerful impact that research dollars have made in my life. I am fundraising for the International Alliance on Progressive MS.

Never before have I had an answer to the question, "how can I help you?" Your donations to the International Alliance on Progressive MS will help me directly.

Vandals

In 1976, when I was nine years old, my mother had us stay with a family after school when she was working.

This family lived very near Kyle school where my brother, Jack, and I had both attended. It was like a cinderblock bunkhouse next to the state police barracks where this family's father was a captain. Kyle school would be repurposed as a morgue after it closed.

Jack and I had a troublemaking friend who also lived nearby. He noticed one day that the door to the shuttered school had been left unlocked, and he let us into the empty building. We ran around like whirling dervishes and got into things like old books and sawdust and soap powders that we spread all around.

Soon after we entered, we heard a whistle downstairs. It sounded like the coaches on the football team blowing and blowing. We realized that we had been caught. The son of the family that we were staying with had called his father at work at the state police headquarters. His father had come over to gather us up and take us back to his house. My father was so angry about this that he made us write letters of apology and spanked us for the last time in my childhood.

25 years later, I would find myself, a fancy lawyer, returning to the state police barracks to interview the police captain and other witnesses in a case that involved the state police.

Wrong Button

What is the simple signal of our age? I clicked the wrong button.

I clicked on the wrong button. Played the wrong program, the wrong song, called the wrong person, for just too long. Our lives are made of buttons. We push them day by day.

A twist on Robert Frosts poem about two paths diverging in a wood.

"Attorney Gilman, have fun in California " Is what the pages said in the cut-out lettering of a ransom note. The pages were sliced in half by a large rusty cleaver. I was drafting a large brief at the end of our mob trial; it was taking me a long time and the witnesses in Providence had referred to me as Attorney Gilman. The box for the cleaver bore a label that had the return address of a prison. The blood was ketchup. It took me about one second to realize what had happened. Attorney Ted Bennett was in the Navy before he came to the law firm to work with me. He believed in good practical jokes. This was my comeuppance after a long-time chasing witnesses with him and trying to deal with the needs and wants of our senior lawyer on the case.

"Going to California" meant being rubbed out by the Providence mob. I laughed deep and long and then finished the brief.

We won the case.

The Candle

The other day Lisa brought me a candle to sit on my warm wood credenza underneath my big TV. I became entranced by this dancing flame. I was doing my meditation app with Sam Harris and found myself looking at the flame. I'm feeling a real increase in concentration. The flame is like one of those silly balloons they have outside of car dealerships that flops and flaps in the breeze. I have it here in my room every day and am looking at it right now as I dictate this post.

My 100th Post

My 100th Post. My last post about the candle was the 100th
post of the blog. I want to take this opportunity to thank all
my loyal readers and especially those at Williams &
Connolly, my Law Firm. Your support and comments have
buoyed me up and encouraged me to keep going with this
blog ever since I started it five years ago. I am working on
taking this product and turning it into a self-published
memoir, so stay tuned for a post about that in the near
future. Thank you. Thank You

As of December, 2021, I have raised $270,000 for the
international alliance on progressive MS. The initial goal was
100,000 but we have shot beyond that. Each $100,000 funds
another researcher for the project. As I told everyone, these
researchers are working on a cure to my version of the
disease. My goal is 1 million, and I am well on my way. I
want to thank the many donors who made this possible,
many from the Law Firm of Williams & Connolly and some
friends here in Seattle. I am overwhelmed by your
generosity and love. Thank you from the bottom of my
heart. So grateful. So fortunate.

2022

Samantha Tubman

Samantha Tubman worked at Williams & Connolly LLP for three years from 2001 to 2004. She was part of the team of paralegals who worked with us on the Vinson Elkins/ Enron matter.

After leaving the firm, Sam went to work for the Obama campaign and then as a staffer in the White House. She was featured in the Washington Post Style Section article titled "Princess of Poise".

When the White House era ended, Michelle Obama picked Sam alone to be the person working with her and setting up the Obama Foundation and other activities. Sam was Director of Special Projects for the Obama Foundation and is now Chief of staff of basketball operations for the LA Lakers.

Sam recently came to Portland, Oregon for a wedding and drove up to see me for the day.

So proud of her.

Scriptural References

Jason Chen is my former trainer and a devout Christian with whom I have shared many kind moments of reflection. Recently, I asked him to please take my blog posts and put each next to a piece of scripture. Thank you, Jason, for this loving and inspiring work.

You will find these Scriptural References in the Appendices and Additional Material Section at the end of this Book.

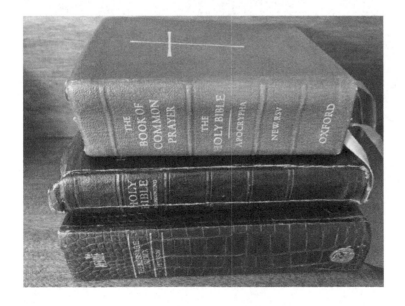

Chumley the Cat

Chumley the cat ate houseflies in my dive apartment in
Spanish Harlem after graduation from Columbia. I was
taking practice tests for the LSAT, and Chumley sat on my
test books like Tiger Woods' father training me to focus. I
would throw him off the book and then he would come right
back. My practice scores improved. I walked over to campus
and sat for the test, earning a perfect score that catapulted
me into Harvard Law School. Thanks, Chumley.

Graceland

My 9-year-old son, Quinn, asked to go somewhere special with me over an important weekend in my 2005 divorce. I asked him where he wanted to go and out of nowhere, he said, "Tennessee." Quinn was an Elvis fan so I said to him, "Quinn, do you want to go to Memphis? Graceland?" And he said "Yes, yes, yes".

Then, the Paul Simon song "Graceland" came into my head: "My traveling companion is nine years old. He is the child of my first marriage. But I've reason to believe, we both will be received in Graceland"

Quinn was the child of my first marriage. At Graceland, Elvis' bed stand had on it two books: Siddhartha, my favorite book of all time, and the Guinness Book of World Records, which was Quinn's favorite book. I knew that I was doing the right thing and also that you just can't make this stuff up.

To Be Continued
I will continue to post occasional blog posts to:
A Fortunate Man with MS 2.0
At:

https://afortunatemanwithms.wordpress.com

Additional Material

Location of videos and speeches referred to in the Chapters of this book:

2014
https://hls.harvard.edu/faculty/directory/10899/Tribe

http://en.wikipedia.org/wiki/Lloyd_Bentsen

https://mssociety.donordrive.com/index.cfm?fuseaction=donorDrive.personalCampaign&participantID=30071

2015: http://www.washingtonpost.com/wp-srv/onpolitics/watergate/Archibald.html

2017: On the Move MS Luncheon

https://www.youtube.com/watch?v=Wmq97Otl02Y&t=7s

Drexel University Graduation Address as given to NW Chapter MS

https://www.youtube.com/watch?v=cFXS1Grxibk&t=2s

2020:

https://www.youtube.com/watch?v=znBqDdaaEyw

Scriptural References

Jason Chen is my former trainer and a devout Christian with whom I have shared many kind moments of reflection. Recently, I asked him to please take my blog posts and put each next to a piece of scripture. Thank you, Jason, for this loving and inspiring work.

The citations are from the *New Revised Standard Version*, Oxford University Press, 1989; and *The Message/REMIX; The Bible in Contemporary Language*, by Eugene Peterson, 2003

2014 Posts

- **August 20th: The Fall**

- 2 Corinthians 12:10

That is why, for Christ's sake, I delight in weaknesses, in insults, in hardships, in persecutions, in difficulties. For when I am weak, then I am strong.

- **August 28th: Laughing and Connecting**

- Philemon 1:7

- Your love has given me great joy and encouragement,

because you, brother, have refreshed the heart of the Lord's people

• **September 6th, 2014: Heat**

• 2 Chronicles 20:17

• You need not fight in this battle; station yourselves, stand and see the salvation of the LORD on your behalf, O Judah and Jerusalem. Do not fear or be dismayed; tomorrow go out to face them, for the LORD is with you

• **September 24th, 2014: MS and the Buddha**

• Proverbs 11:1

• A false balance is an abomination to the Lord, but a just weight is his delight

• **September 28th, 2014: The Community of Now**

• Psalm 127:3-5

• Children are a heritage from the Lord, offspring a reward from him. Like arrows in the hands of a warrior are children born in one's youth. Blessed is the man whose quiver is full of them. They will not put to shame when they contend with their opponents in court.

• **October 25, 2014: The Goal is No Longer Health but Beauty**

- Psalm 62:1

- "Truly my soul finds rest in God; my salvation comes from Him"

- **October 26, 2014: The Question**

- Jeremiah 29:11

- "For I know the plans I have for you," declares the LORD, "plans to prosper you and not to harm you, plans to give you hope and a future"

- **December 6th, 2014: A Christmas Miracle**

- James 1:17

- "Every good gift and every perfect gift is from above, coming down from the Father of lights with whom there is no variation or shadow due to change."

- **December 14, 2014: The Ghost of ChristMaS Presence**

- Isaiah 64:8

- "But now, O Lord, you are our Father; we are the clay, and you are the potter; we are all the work of your hand"

2015 Posts

- **January 25th: On Board**

- Galatians 6:2

- Carry each other's burdens, and in this way you will fulfill the law of Christ

- **February 8th, 2015: The Day We First Met and the Dance Began**

- Joshua 1:9

- Have I not commanded you? Be strong and courageous. Do not be afraid; do not be discouraged, for the Lord your God will be with you wherever you go.

- **March 2nd, 2015: Today I Bought a Wheelchair. It's Okay, and I May Even Walk More Because of it**

- 2 Corinthians 5:17

- Therefore, if anyone is in Christ, he is a new creation. The old has passed away; behold, the new has come.

- **May 11th, 2015: Enormous Support at The Dinner of Champions**

- James 1:12

- Blessed is the man who remains steadfast under trial, for when he has stood the test he will receive the crown of life, which God has promised to those who love him.

- **June 19th, 2015: When You are "Certain," Think Again,**

and then Laugh

• Romans 12:3

• For by the grace given to me I say to everyone among you not to think of himself more highly than he ought to think, but to think with sober judgement, each according to the measure of faith that God has assigned

• **July 1st, 2015: Heat**

• Isaiah 4:6

• There will be a shelter to give shade from the heat by day, and refuge and protection from the storm and the rain.

• **August 1st, 2015: When Illusion Ends, What Rushes in? Terror, then hopefully the calming sea**

• John 14:27

• Peace I leave with you; my peace I give to you. Not as the world gives do I give to you. Let not your hearts be troubled, neither let them be afraid

• **August 25th, 2015: 50 Shades of Greenman**

• 2 Corinthians 4:17-18

• For our light and momentary troubles are achieving for us an eternal glory that far outweighs them all. So we fix our eyes not on what is seen, but what is unseen, since what is seen is temporary but what is unseen is eternal.

• **October 4th, 2015: Gil as Green Lantern**

• John 15:13

• Greater love has no one than this, that someone lay down his life for his friends

• **November 9th, 2015: A Little Stress Relief**

• Matthew 13:32

• It is the smallest of all seeds, but when it has grown it is larger than all the garden plants and becomes a tree, so that the birds of the air come and make nests in its branches

• **November 26th, 2015: It Happened on a Grimy New York Subway in 1985**

• 2 Corinthians 9:11

• You will be enriched in every way so that you can be generous on every occasion and through us your generosity will result in thanksgiving to God

• **December 15th, 2015: The Ribs that Saved Christmas: How I Broke Five Ribs and Learned the Holiday's True Meaning**

• Jeremiah 17:14

• Heal me, O Lord, and I shall be healed; save me, and I shall be saved, for you are my praise

2016 Posts

• **January 6th, 2016: It's Time. Time for the Hardest Part. So Let's Roll**

• Isaiah 41:10

• Fear not, I am with you; be not dismayed, for I am your God; I will strengthen you, I will help you, I will uphold you with my righteous right hand.

• **January 24th, 2016: The First Day with My New Electric Wheelchair**

• Philippians 4:19

• And my God will supply every need of yours according to his riches in glory in Jesus Christ

• **February 6th, 2016: A Sign for a Broken Record**

• 1 Corinthians 2:9

• Eye has not seen, nor ear heard, nor have entered into the heart of man the things which God has prepared for those who love him.

• **February 18th, 2016: Walk/Run MS is Approaching. The GREEN MANiacs Are Gathering…..**

• Ephesians 3:14-15

• For this reason I kneel before the Father, from whom every family in heaven and on earth derives its name

• **March 19th, 2016: Guess what came out of the mud?**

• Isaiah 28:16

• So this is what the Sovereign LORD says: "See, I lay a stone in Zion, a tested stone, a precious cornerstone for a sure foundation; the one relies on it will never be stricken with panic

• **April 24, 2016: Inspiration on a Newark New Jersey flight to DC**

• Galatians 6:2

• Carry each other's burdens and so will fulfill the law of Christ

• **June 6th, 2016: The Spirit Award, May 14th, 2016**

• 1 John 4:13

• By this we know that we abide in Him and He in us, because he has given us of his Spirit

• **June 9th, 2016: Video of Speeches in Seattle**

• Proverbs 19:21

• Many are the plans in a person's heart, but it is the Lord's purpose that prevails

• **June 22nd, 2016: Some Good News from an Old Buddy**

• 1 Thessalonians 5:18

• Be thankful in all circumstances, for this is God's will for you who belong to Christ Jesus

• **July 21st, 2016: To Be Known and to be Loved, A Poem**

• 1 John 4:18

• There is no fear in love. But perfect love drives out fear, because fear has to do with punishment. The one who fears is not made perfect in love.

• **August 6th, 2016: At Last a Disease Modifying Therapy**

• Psalm 9:10

• "And those who know your name put their trust in you, for you, O Lord, have not forsaken those who seek you."

• **August 24th, 2016: 11:17am**

• Ezra 3:11

• With praise and thanksgiving they sang to the Lord:

"He is good; His love towards Israel endures forever"

And all the people gave a great shout of praise to the Lord, because the foundation of the house of the Lord was laid

- **September 22nd, 2016: The Story No One Want to Read**

- John 16:33

- "I have told you these things, so that in me you may have peace. In this world you will have trouble. But take heart! I have overcome the world."

- **October 23rd, 2016: An Urban Symphony with Extra Needles**

- Isaiah 26:3

- "You keep him in perfect peace whose mind is stayed on you, because he trusts in you "

- **November 26th, 2016: Gratitude Showers Our Lives with Grace**

- 2 Thessalonians 1:3

- "We ought always to give thanks to God for you, brothers, as is right, because your faith is growing abundantly, and the love of every one of you for one another is increasing."

- **December 9th, 2016**

- 2 Peter 1:5-7

• "For this very reason, make every effort to add to your faith goodness; and to goodness, knowledge; and to knowledge, self-control; and to self-control, perseverance; and to perseverance, godliness; and to godliness, mutual affection; and to mutual affection, love."

2017 Posts

• **January 7th, 2017: Mindful Through Terror**

• Colossians 3:2

• Set your minds on things that are above, not on things that are on earth

• **January 22nd, 2017: Delight**

• James 5:13

• Is anyone among you suffering? Let him pray. Is anyone cheerful? Let him sing praise

• **April 1st, 2017: The "New" Drug for Progressive MS**

• Proverbs 25:25

• Like cold water to a weary soul, so is good news from a distant land

• **April 11th, 2017: Keynote at Graduation for Doctors of Physical Therapy at Drexel U**

• 2 Corinthians 12:9-10

• But he said to me, "My grace is sufficient for you, for my power is made perfect in weakness." Therefore I will boast all the more gladly of my weaknesses, so that the power of Christ may rest upon me. For the sake of Christ, then I am content with weaknesses, insults, hardships, persecutions, and calamities. For when I am weak, then I am strong.

• **May 3rd, 2017: Keynote Address at Drexel University Graduation for Doctors of Physical Therapy, April 7th, 2017, as given to staff at NW Chapter of the MS Society**

• 1 Peter 3:8

• Finally, all of you, be like-minded, be sympathetic, love one another, be compassionate and humble

• **June 22nd, 2017: Get Busy Living**

• Psalm 37:4

• Delight yourself in the lord, and he will give you the desires of your heart

• **August 1st, 2017: Is this the end?**

• Romans 5:3-5

• More than that, we rejoice in our sufferings, knowing that suffering produces endurance, and endurance produces character, and character produces hope, and hope does not put us to shame, because God's love has been poured into our hearts through the Holy Spirit who has been given to us.

- **October 18th, 2017: The Master in the Kitchen**

- Ephesians 4:29

- Let no corrupting talk come out of your mouths, but only such as is good for building up, as fits the occasion, that it may give grace to those who hear

- **November 13th, 2017: Five Minute Speech to 850 People at MS Society's One the Move Lunch, Seattle 10/26/17**

- Proverbs 18:16

- A gift opens the way and ushers the giver into the presence of the great.

- **November 28th, 2017: Cul-de-sacs**

- Proverbs 4:23

- Keep your heart with all vigilance, for from it flow the springs of life

- **December 12th, 2017: A Christmas Miracle**

- Mark 10:27

- Jesus looked at them and said, "With man this is impossible, but not with God; all things are possible with

God."

- **December 23rd, 2017: A Beautiful Thought**

- 1 John 5:14

- This is the confidence we have in approaching God: that if we ask anything according to his will, He hears us

- **December 25th, 2017: Holiness Today**

- Matthew 6:26

- Look at the birds of the air; they neither sow nor reap nor gather into barns, and yet your heavenly Father feeds them. Are you not of more value than they?

2018 Posts

- **January 16th, 2018: All Will be Well**

- Psalm 46:10

- Be still and know that I am God. I will be exalted among the nations, I will be exalted in the earth!

- **February 2nd, 2018: It Happened at the Seattle Women's March**

- Galatians 3:28

- There is neither Jew nor Greek, there is neither slave nor

free, there is no male and female, for you are all one in Christ
Jesus

• **February 25th, 2018: Gratitude**

• Hebrews 12:28

• Therefore let us be grateful for receiving a kingdom that
cannot be shaken, and thus let us offer to God acceptable
worship, with reverence and awe

• **April 20th, 2018: Not MS?**

• Proverbs 17:22

• A joyful heart is good medicine, but a crushed spirit dries
up the bones

• **April 29th, 2018: Samurai**

• Ruth 1:16-17

• But Ruth said, "Do not urge me to leave you or to return
from following you. For where you go I will go, and where
you lodge I will lodge. Your people shall be my people, and
your God my God. Where you die I will die, and there will I
be buried. May the Lord do so to me and more also if
anything but death parts me from you."

• **July 30th, 2018: Lessons from Mister Rogers**

• 2 Corinthians 1:12

• For our boast is this, the testimony of our conscience, that we behaved in the world with simplicity and godly sincerity, not by earthly wisdom but by the grace of God, and supremely so toward you.

• **November 16th, 2018: The Swallow Battle**

• James 1:2-4

• Count it all joy, my brothers, when you meet trials of various kinds, for you know that the testing of your faith produces steadfastness. And let steadfastness have its full effect, that you may be perfect and complete, lacking in nothing.

• **November 23rd, 2018: No pain no pain**

• Ephesians 5:20

• Giving thanks always and for everything to God the Father in the name of our Lord Jesus Christ

2019 Posts

• **January 22nd, 2019: The Old Street**

• Proverbs 24:16

• For the righteous falls seven times and rises again, but the wicked stumble in times of calamity

• **June 19th, 2019: Purpose**

• Philippians 4:6-7

• Do not be anxious about anything, but in everything by prayer and supplication with thanksgiving let your requests be made known to God. And the peace of God, which surpasses all understanding, will guard your hearts and your minds in Christ Jesus.

• **July 25th, 2019: Let's Dance**

• Then David said to Solomon his son, "Be strong and courageous and do it. Do not be afraid and do not be dismayed, for the Lord God, even my God, is with you. He will not leave you or forsake you, until all the work for the service of the house of the Lord is finished.

• **September 19th, 2019: Our Summer on the Bay Downtown**

• Hebrews 11:6

• And without faith it is impossible to please him, for whoever would draw near to God must believe that he exists and that he rewards those who seek him.

• **October 9th, 2019: Reasons for Optimism**

• Romans 15:13

• May the God of hope fill you with all joy and peace as you trust in Him, so that you may overflow with hope by the power of the Holy Spirit

- **December 18th, 2019: One Day in the Senate Impeachment Trial, 1998**

- Philippians 3:13-14

- Brothers, I do not consider that I have made it my own. But one thing I do: forgetting what lies behind and straining forward to what lies ahead, I press on toward the goal for the prize of the upward call of God in Christ Jesus

2020 Posts

- **January 17th, 2020: We Here Know Why Honor Matters**

- Hebrews 13:18

- Pray for us, for we are sure that we have a clear conscience, desiring to act honorably in all things.

- **February 6th, 2020: We Spoke to the Mafia Lawyer as the Sun Set Blood Red Out His Office Window Over Hoboken**

- 1 John 5:4

- For everyone who has been born of God overcomes the world. And this is the victory that has overcome the world — our faith.

- **March 5th, 2020: GREENMANiacs Mswalk link**

- Ecclesiastes 4:9-12

• Two are better than one, because they have a good reward for their toil. For if they fall, one will lift up his fellow. But woe to him who is alone when he falls and has not another to lift him up! Again, if two lie together, they keep warm, but how can one keep warm alone? And though a man might prevail against one who is alone, two will withstand him — a threefold cord is not quickly broken.

• **March 5th, 2020: GREENMANiacs MS Walk**

• James 2:14-26

• What good is it, my brothers, if someone says he has faith but does not have works? Can that faith save him? If a brother or sister is poorly clothed and lacking in daily food, and one of you says to them, "Go in peace, be warmed and filled," without giving them the things needed for the body, what good is that? So also faith by itself, if it does not have works, is dead. But someone will say, "You have faith and I have works." Show me your faith apart from your works, and I will show you my faith by my works. …

• **May 28th, 2020: What Can We Do?**

• Colossians 3:12

• Put on then, as God's chosen ones, holy and beloved, compassionate hearts, kindness, humility, meekness, and patience

• **May 30th, 2020: Thank You**

• Colossians 3:17

• And whatever you do, in word or deed, do everything in the name of the Lord Jesus, giving thanks to God the Father through him.

• **June 24th, 2020**

• Luke 13:24

• Strive to enter through the narrow door. For many, I tell you, will seek to enter and will not be able.

• **July 14th, 2020: I Stood Up!**

• Matthew 17:20

• He said to them, "Because of your little faith. For truly, I say to you, if you have faith like a grain of mustard seed, you will say to this mountain, 'Move from here to there,' and it will move, and nothing will be impossible for you."

• **August 6th, 2020: What We See**

• Proverbs 15:3

• The eyes of the Lord are in every place, keeping watch on the evil and the good

• **September 22nd, 2020: Rules of the 100 Year Flood**

• John 14:15

• If you love me, you will keep my commandments

- **October 20th, 2020: Combat Meditation**

- Psalm 19:14

- Let the words of my mouth and the meditation of my heart be acceptable in your sight, O Lord, my rock and my redeemer

- **November 17th, 2020: Ton of Bricks**

- Romans 8:18

- For I consider that the sufferings of this present time are not worth comparing with the glory that is to be revealed to us

- **December 1st, 2020: Vulnerability**

- 2 Corinthians 12:9

- But he said to me, "My grace is sufficient for you, for my power is made perfect in weakness." Therefore I will boast all the more gladly of my weaknesses, so that the power of Christ may rest upon me.

- **December 3rd, 2020: Best Lawyer Joke Ever**

- Psalm 126:2

- Then our mouth was filled with laughter, and our tongue with shouts of joy; then they said among the nations, "The Lord has done great things for them."

- **December 8th, 2020: Never Surrender**

- Hebrews 12:1

- Therefore, since we are surrounded by so great a cloud of witnesses, let us also lay aside every weight, and sin which clings so closely, and let us run with endurance the race that is set before us

- **December 10th, 2020: First Story of Overcoming**

- Isaiah 55:8-9

- For my thoughts are not your thoughts, neither are your ways my ways, declares the Lord. For as the heavens are higher than the earth, so are my ways higher than your ways and my thoughts than your thoughts.

2021 Posts

- **January 12th, 2021: Sweet Dog Story**

- 1 Corinthians 13:4-7

- Love is patient and kind; love does not envy or boast; it is not arrogant or rude. It does not insist on its own way; it is not irritable or resentful; it does not rejoice at wrongdoing but rejoices with the truth. Love bears all things, believes all things, hopes all things, endures all things.

- **January 18th, 2021: Ballard Landmark, Long Term Care, On Friday**

- Romans 8:28

- And we know that for those who love God all things work together for good, for those who are called according to his purpose.

- **February 18th, 2021: A Unicorn**

- Matthew 7:7

- "Ask, and it will be given to you; seek, and you will find; knock, and it will be opened to you.

- **March 23rd, 2021: Shotgun Shack**

- Job 11:18

- And you will feel secure, because there is hope; you will look around and take your rest in security.

- **April 15th, 2021: Miracle Worker**

- Acts 4:30

- While you stretch out your hand to heal, and signs and wonders are performed through the name of your holy servant Jesus.

- **June 3rd, 2021: Luxury**

- Numbers 6:24-26

• The Lord bless you and keep you; the Lord make his face to shine upon you and be gracious to you; the Lord lift up his countenance upon you and give you peace.

• **June 8th, 2021: Please Contribute**

• Acts 20:35

• In all things I have shown you that by working hard in this way we must help the weak and remember the words of the Lord Jesus, how he himself said, 'It is more blessed to give than to receive.

• **July 1st, 2021: Vandals**

• Proverbs 16:9

• The heart of man plans his way, but the Lord establishes his steps

• **August 26th, 2021: Wrong Button**

• Psalm 119:105

• Your word is a lamp to my feet and a light to my path.

ABOUT THE AUTHOR

After graduating with high honors from the Harvard Law
School in 1994 and clerking on federal district and circuit
courts, Gil worked on litigation matters as an associate and
partner at the Washington, DC law firm, Williams &
Connolly LLP, from 1996 to 2010. His cases included
assisting in the firm's defense of former President Bill
Clinton in investigations and the Senate Impeachment trial,
individual-volunteer representation of former Vice President
Al Gore in the 2000 election crisis, defense of a union
president against charges of association with organized
crime, and more than six years representing a
professional firm in the Enron matter.

Gil ended legal practice in 2010 and currently assists the firm
with the training of younger lawyers and with issues
involving electronic discovery.

Born in Massachusetts in 1967, Gil grew up in South
Charleston, West Virginia, and moved to Bellevue,

Washington, where he attended Interlake High School,
graduating in 1985. He attended Columbia University in
New York City and worked in Manhattan as a legal
assistant. In 1994, in his third year at Harvard
Law School, Gil was diagnosed with multiple sclerosis.